25 WALKS

DEESIDE

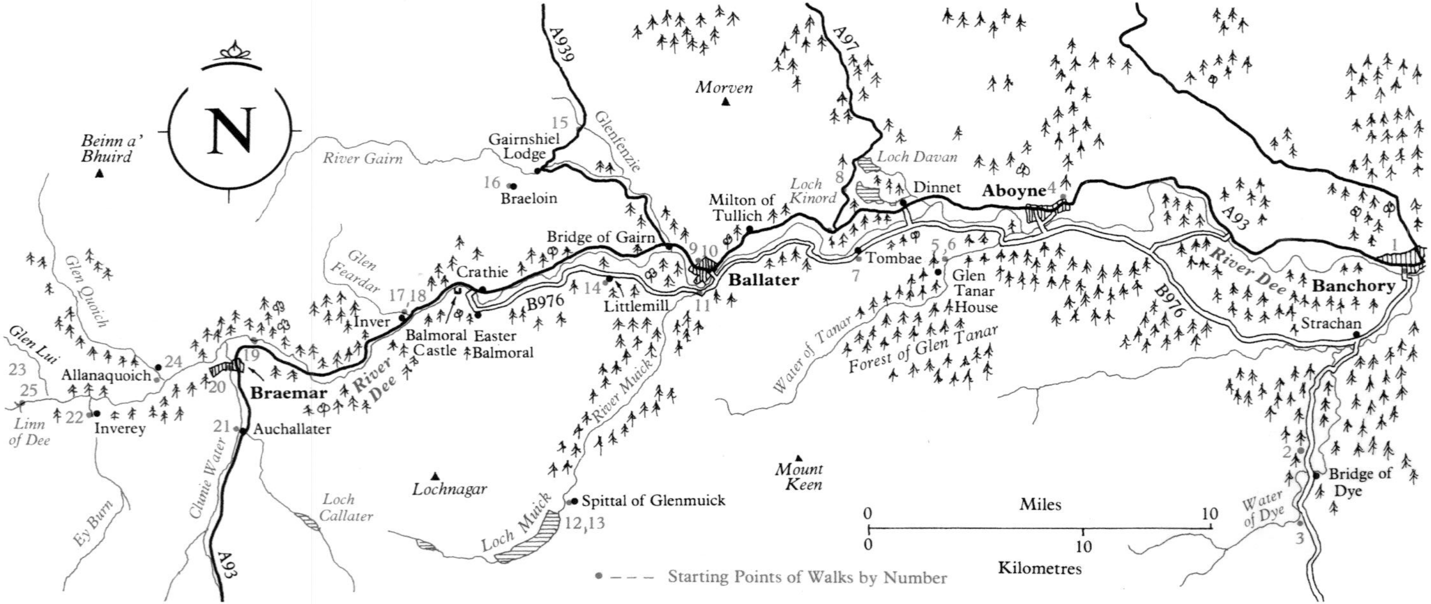
N
Beinn a' Bhuird
River Gairn
A939
15
Glenfenzie
Gairnshiel Lodge
16
Braeloin
Morven
A97
Loch Davan
8
Loch Kinord
Dinnet
Aboyne
4
Milton of Tullich
Bridge of Gairn
9
10
Ballater
Tombae
7
5,6
Glen Tanar House
A93
River Dee
Banchory
1
Strachan
B976
Glen Quoich
Glen Feardar
Crathie
17,18
Inver
Balmoral Castle
Easter Balmoral
14
Littlemill
11
Water of Tanar
Forest of Glen Tanar
Glen Lui
23
25
Allanaquoich
24
19
20
Braemar
River Dee
Linn of Dee
22
Inverey
21
Auchallater
River Muick
Mount Keen
Lochnagar
Loch Callater
Clunie Water
Ey Burn
Loch Muick
Spittal of Glenmuick
12,13
A93
2
Bridge of Dye
Water of Dye
3
Miles
0
10
0
10
Kilometres
Starting Points of Walks by Number

25 WALKS

DEESIDE

Robert Smith

Revised by Peter Dawes and Alistair Mackenzie

Series Editor: Roger Smith

mercatpress

www.mercatpress.com

First published 1994
Revised editions published 1995, 1999
This revised edition published 2005
Mercat Press Ltd., 10 Coates Crescent, Edinburgh EH3 7AL
© Mercat Press 2005
ISBN 184183 0763

Acknowledgements

The authors and editor gratefully acknowledge the help of the National
Trust for Scotland, Scottish Natural Heritage, Tourist Information
Centres (VisitScotland) and the Upper Deeside Access Trust in the
preparation of this revised edition.
Photographs are by Robert Smith and Peter Dawes.

All facts have been checked as far as possible but the authors, editor and
publisher cannot be held responsible for any errors, however caused.

Cartography new to this edition by MapSet Ltd., Newcastle upon Tyne
Reproduced by permission of Ordnance Survey on behalf of
The Controller of Her Majesty's Stationery Office
© Crown Copyright 2005
Ordnance Survey Licence number 100031557

Printed and bound by Bell & Bain Ltd., Glasgow

CONTENTS

USEFUL INFORMATION

The length of each walk is given in kilometres and miles, but within the text measurements are metric for simplicity. The walks are described in detail and are supported by accompanying maps (study them before you start the walk), so there should be little likelihood of getting lost, but if you want a back-up you will find the 1:50,000 Landranger or 1:25,000 Pathfinder Ordnance Survey maps on sale locally.

Legislation confirmed by the Scottish Parliament in 2005 means that there is now a general right of access to open countryside in Scotland, but this right should be exercised responsibly. On all walks please respect the Country Code. Its most important provisions include carefully closing all gates behind you (assuming you have to open them), being scrupulous about not dropping litter, and avoiding unnecessary noise. If you have a dog, make sure it is under control – keep it on the lead in areas where there may be deer, grouse or other wildlife, or farm livestock.

Every care has been taken to make the descriptions and maps as accurate as possible, but the author and publishers can accept no responsibility for errors, however caused. The countryside is always changing and there will inevitably be alterations to some aspects of these walks as time goes by. The publishers and authors would be happy to receive comments and suggested alterations for future editions of the book.

Helpful websites

VisitScotland – *www.visitscotland.com*.
Upper Deeside Access Trust – *www.udat.co.uk*.
National Trust for Scotland – *www.nts.org.uk*.
Cairngorms National Park – *www.cairngorms.co.uk*.

By keying the town name e.g. 'Braemar' or 'Ballater' into a search engine you will often be led to community websites which contain a lot of helpful information.

METRIC MEASUREMENTS

At the beginning of each walk, the distance is given in miles and kilometres. Within the text, all measurements are metric for simplicity (Ordnance Survey maps are also now all metric). However, a conversion table might be still be useful.

The basic statistic to remember is that one kilometre is five-eighths of a mile. Half a mile is equivalent to 800 metres and a quarter-mile is 400 metres. Below that distance, yards and metres are little different in practical terms.

km	miles
1	0.625
1.6	1
2	1.25
3	1.875
3.2	2
4	2.5
4.8	3
5	3.125
6	3.75
6.4	4
7	4.375
8	5
9	5.625
10	6.25
16	10

INTRODUCTION

Royal Deeside is a walker's paradise – the 'dear Paradise' that Queen Victoria discovered when she came north in the mid 19th century to make Balmoral her Scottish home. It is a land of magnificent mountains and romantic glens, and it is also castle country, with a rich and colourful history. This book takes you on 25 Deeside walks, from Banchory near Aberdeen to Braemar and the edge of the Cairngorm Mountains.

It gives you a taste of the wild places, but you don't have to be a hardened hillwalker or Munro-bagger to enjoy it. The walks are well within the capability of anyone who is reasonably fit, and most are suitable for children. They range in length from 6 to 16 kilometres (4 to 10 miles).

The weather in this part of Scotland, particularly as you get near to the hills, can be changeable, so you should go dressed for whatever Nature offers. Waterproofs are advised for all the walks – just in case. For many of them strong walking shoes or hill boots are necessary. Information at the beginning of each walk gives advice on clothing and footwear.

Part of the pleasure of walking is in knowing about the countryside around you ... its history, its flora and fauna, its myths and legends. This book takes you on the trail of the Haunted Stag, along a wooded track of the Warlock's Stone, and up by 'lonely, lovely dark Loch Kander'. You will cross the Seven Brigs, and search for the Seven Wells.

Deer stalking and grouse shooting take place over some of the hill areas covered in this book. These activities, as well as being essential for the good management of deer and grouse (and the heather on which the latter depend for food) provide both income and employment, and it is important to take due precaution during the shooting season.

The main period of activity is from mid-August to late October. During this period it is advisable to keep to the main paths and tracks so that minimum disturbance is caused. Further advice on areas where shooting and stalking takes place can be obtained from estate offices or tourist information centres.

Much of the area covered by the book is also covered by the East Grampian Deer Management Group, a voluntary grouping of estates. You will find their attractive and informative stone signs in a number of places. These signs include a map showing the preferred walking routes during the shooting season.

Parts of the area are also covered by the Upper Deeside Access Trust, which is doing splendid work on opening up path networks and restoring old paths and rights of way. UDAT have produced a number of walks leaflets which are available locally. You can get more information from their website, *www.udat.co.uk*.

We hope you enjoy following these walks as much as we have enjoyed putting them together.

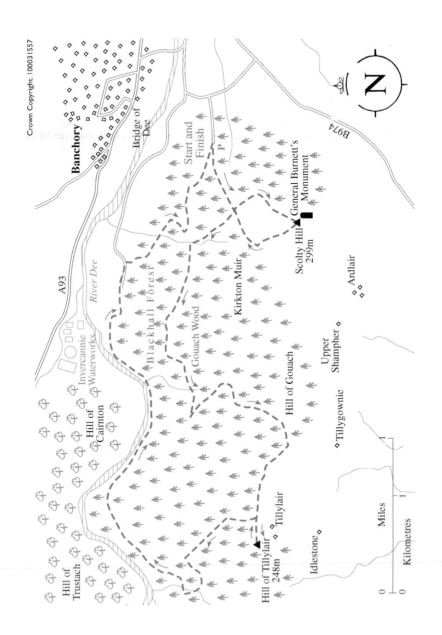

Crown Copyright. 10003 1557

SCOLTY AND TILLYLAIR

colty Hill, on the outskirts of Banchory, might have remained a small and undistinguished peak if someone hadn't put a tower on top of it. That was in 1842, when the tower was erected in memory of General William Burnett of Banchory Lodge. Since then, Scolty's tower has been a familiar landmark on Lower Deeside and a favourite walk for both locals and visitors. As the Forestry Commission is encouraging more use of the woodland park for recreation, this walk extends from Scolty to another fine viewpoint and an attractive riverside walk.

From the car park, go through the barrier on the forest road and walk on following the white arrows up to a kissing gate and crossroads just beyond. Turn left here and after about 150m, take the rough path on the right which leads uphill through open woodlands of birch, interspersed with Scots pine. The track gets steeper and

INFORMATION

Distance 15 km (9 miles) circular.

Start and finish Scolty woodland car park. From Banchory's Dee Street (B974) car park, cross the Bridge of Dee and shortly turn sharp right, up the Auchattie road. Follow the woodland park signs to the car park amongst the trees.

Terrain Generally good tracks, roughish in places, boots or strong shoes recommended.

Refreshments Wide choice in Banchory.

Toilets In Banchory, none on the route.

Information Tourist Information Centre in Scott Skinner Square, off High Street in Banchory.

Scolty Tower

stonier the higher you climb and finally leaves the trees to emerge at the tower on the bare Scolty plateau.

Two indicators near the tower pick out the distant hills and a handful of lesser peaks, while nearer to hand, Banchory lies below, stretching out from the winding Dee. This Deeside town, almost a dormitory for Aberdeen nowadays, must have been a good deal smaller and less lively when the tower was erected by General Burnett's 'numerous friends and tenantry'. He was a veteran of the Napoleonic War and had died three years earlier, in 1839, at the age of 72. Not much has been written about him, but he was said to be 'a public spirited gentleman and a kind landlord, whose memory will be long and gratefully cherished in this neighbourhood'.

The tower now has a metal spiral staircase inside and a plaque on the tower commemorates a visit by the Prince of Wales on 15 September 1992.

Scolty tower looks out across the vast expanse of Blackhall Forest, covering some 1200 hectares, which was planted by the Forestry Commission to replace large-scale felling by Canadian lumberjacks during the Second World War. As the forest is now largely mature, felling takes place from time to time, but diversions are usually put in place, and a bonus is that new views are being opened up throughout the forest.

Go past the tower and follow a path dropping down the west side of the hill and circling round to reach the crossroads at the kissing gate on the outward route. Turn left here on a footpath which, after another kissing gate, shortly becomes a wider forest road. Ignore a track to the left and at a T-junction turn left up a main forest road. After some twists and turns, you will reach a fork with an information board on the right. Take left here and shortly again left uphill, climbing steadily across the shoulder of Hill of Gouach. Keep on the main road ignoring tracks to right and left, and eventually drop downhill with views opening up to Feughside and the hills beyond.

Beyond a large field on the left, the track swings right and here you may wish to follow a pleasant little path through the pines to the left for about 300m to the

River Dee at Blackhall

triangulation pillar on Hill of Tillylair. On returning, continue downhill, go straight across at a crossroads on to a walkers-only track, and in 60m turn left down a narrow footpath beside a stone dyke. There are glimpses of the river Dee ahead as you descend. Cross a forest track with steps at each side and eventually the footpath swings left and widens. At a T-junction, turn right downhill and go straight on, ignoring a main track to the right, and eventually reach a fire pond on your left. A short distance takes you to the riverbank and an attractive walk downstream. The large white building on the opposite bank is Cairnton House and just past here is a bouldery stretch of river called the 'Glisters'. In the days when timber was brought down river in log rafts, this was one of the most difficult parts of the journey.

Once through a gate, you leave the river and pass Glenbogle Lodge, a large wooden building on your right, and follow the lodge drive until you meet the public road. The buildings on the right were the stables for the now demolished Blackhall Castle, a castellated mansion similar to Balmoral. The old walled garden can be seen through the trees to the left. About 200m along the tarred road, just before a steading conversion, turn right through a barrier on to a stony track. At the fork, take left and proceed on until you reach a triangular junction. Bend left here and after 60m take the left track. Further on, a narrow path is signposted into the wood on the right and by following this path, going left and right when you reach a stone dyke, you will end up opposite the car park.

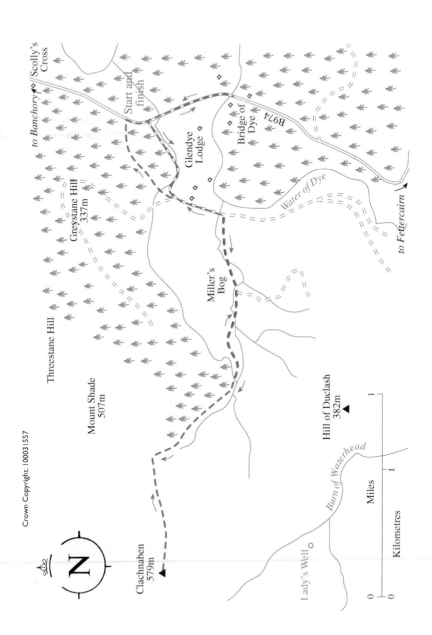

CLACHNABEN AND BRIDGE OF DYE

Clachnaben, near the northern end of the Cairn o'Mounth pass, is one of the best-loved hills on Lower Deeside. Its 29m high wart-like tor is a prominent feature seen from the surrounding countryside, but can also be seen from a greater distance, as the old rhyme indicates.

> *Clochnaben and Bennachie*
> *Are twa' landmarks frae the sea.*

This walk starts near the foot of the Cairn o' Mounth pass which has always been, and still is, a busy route for travellers. Edward the First of England, the Hammer of the Scots, led his invading troops over the pass during the Wars of Independence, and later it became a favourite haunt of bandits who robbed and murdered travellers making their way along its danger-fraught miles. The Cairn o' Mounth was also one of the most important routes for the great cattle treks which brought the drovers and their herds from the north to the major cattle trysts at Brechin, Falkirk and Perth.

Leaving the car park, walk south down the road for 400m to see one of the oldest, and finest, bridges on Deeside. The Bridge of Dye has survived well over 300 winters and looks as sturdy today as it did when it was built by Sir Alexander Fraser of Durris in 1681. The Dye can be at

INFORMATION

Distance: 8km (5miles) circular.

Start and finish: Car park in quarry (GR649868). Take the B974 from Banchory to Strachan and turn left over the bridge as you enter Strachan (signed Fettercairn). The car park is 400m before Bridge of Dye – 7km (4miles) from Strachan on the right among beech trees.

Terrain: Good track all the way, roughish in places. Boots or strong shoes recommended.

Refreshments: None on route, nearest in Banchory.

Toilets: None on route.

Bridge of Dye

times an angry river. Indeed, an Act of Parliament said the bridge stood upon 'one of the most impetuous waters within the Kingdom', and when a move was made to introduce a toll on the bridge in 1685, a petition said that there were times when the Water of Dye 'damnifies the bridge exceedingly'. Damnified or not, it survived even the Muckle Spate of 1829 which brought down many other bridges throughout the area.

A relic of the days of toll charges can be seen on the crown of the bridge. Two pillars facing each other across the carriageway have sockets in them, from which was suspended a chain to block the road. A more recent way of controlling the traffic using the road is recalled by the concrete pillboxes on each side just before the bridge – relics of World War Two.

Leaving the bridge, retrace your steps back along the road and opposite the Old Smithy Cottage, turn left through a barrier and up a wide track with lovely old trees on both sides. You are now walking in the Glen Dye part of Fasque Estate which has belonged to the Gladstone family since 1829. A younger son of the first of the Gladstone lairds, Sir John, was William Ewart Gladstone who became a prominent 19th-century Liberal states-man, serving four different spells as Prime Minister. His descendants still live in Fasque House near Fettercairn.

On reaching the end of the wood, with a wide view of the hills ahead, turn left and go down past the entrance to the estate office and workshops until you reach a wooden bridge over a burn. Immediately past the bridge, swing right on the track facing towards Clachnaben and cross three bridges until you reach a gate near the corner of a wood with an information board beyond. This tells you about the Clachnaben Path Trust, formed in 1997, which has done outstanding work on what was becoming a very eroded path to the top of the hill.

Follow the delightful path on the left edge of the wood and eventually you will emerge on to the open hillside and a good pull up to the top. The impressive dry ravine on your right, between Clachnaben and Mount Shade, is known locally as the Devil's Bite, and there is more devilish work higher up. Especially on the higher reaches of the path, there are some fine examples of 'pitching', making a stone staircase to reach the tor which

The summit tor on Clachnaben

can be ascended by going round the back and scrambling up some large boulders. Rock climbers can sometimes be seen on the steep face of the tor, and the view is extensive with cars crawling up the Cairn o' Mounth road appearing very small against the rolling moors.

The name Clachnaben means 'the stone of the mountain' and tradition attributes the presence of the tor to a quarrel between the Devil and his wife. A poem by the Rev George Kennedy of Birse near Aboyne, who died in 1789, says the stone lay 'low in a plain' before being picked up by the Devil. A more recent poem by Joseph Knowles describes what happened next.

"Have at you now, you beldame" roared the Fiend,
And hurled the rock through the resounding skies;
Dreadful it fell, and crushed his breathless friend,
And there entombed Her Hellish Highness lies.

Retrace your steps all the way back, past the estate office entrance, and at the corner of the stone dyke go across on to a path, climbing up into the wood, which will take you back to the car park in the quarry.

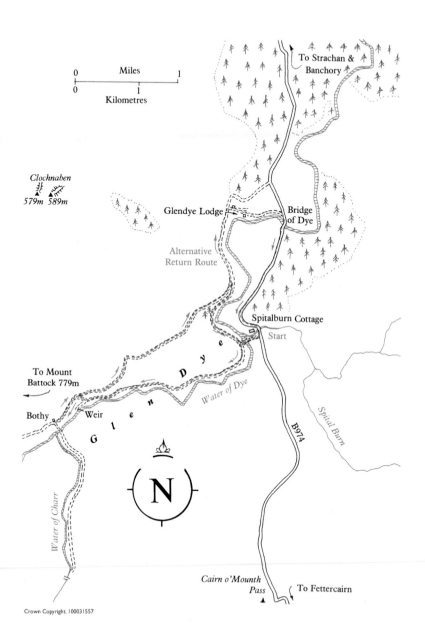

GLEN DYE

The giant tor on the 579m Clachnaben, south of the Deeside village of Strachan (pronounced Stra-an), can be seen from most parts of Lower Deeside. Its wart-like rock, 29m high, looks down on the Cairn o' Mounth pass, which for centuries has been a main artery from Deeside to the south. Ten kilometres from Strachan the road crosses a bridge spanning the Spital Burn, a tributary of the Water of Dye. Here, as the name Spital indicates, there was once a hospice serving travellers going over the Cairn o'Mounth. Now there is only a ruined cottage, but this tranquil spot is the starting point of a walk through a glen whose scenery is in sharp contrast to the naked moors around Clachnaben. There is an old ballad which says:

> The Caim-na-Mounth is bleak and bare
> An' cauld is Cloch-na-bane.

The Spital wasn't always tranquil. The hospice later became a public house, a haunt of thieves, and robberies were common on the highway, but in time the intimation was made in Strachan church: 'The Cairn o'Mounth road is quite safe now. There's honest folk at the Spital'.

Just past the Spital bridge, on the right-hand side of the road, a track goes down about 200m to a fence and locked gate. The fence is surmounted by a high, awkward stile. Take care going over it. Once on the other side, a sturdy bridge crosses the Water of Dye and a short distance further on, the track meets up with another coming in on the right from Glendye Lodge. Turn left here.

The route follows the river, with woods and pleasant haughland below. This is what Joseph Grant, a well-known Deeside writer, had in mind in 1869 when he wrote about 'the beautiful valley of Glen Dye – an oasis in a desert'. But the 'matchless' scenery gradually gives way to moorland. On the right, where a gap in the hills opens up a view of Clachnaben, a solitary tree can be seen in the middle of an area where there are crumbling stone dykes and the ruins of a cottage.

INFORMATION

Distance: 8km (5 miles) circular,

Start and Finish: Spital Burn (GR 647847). Take B974 from Banchory to Strachan and turn left over the bridge as you enter Strachan (signed to Fettercairn). Spital Burn is about 10km (6 miles) from Strachan.

Terrain: Good tracks all the way. Boots or strong shoes recommended. Take waterproof and warm clothing with you.

Refreshments: None on route. Take food and drink with you. There is a seasonal cafe at Clatterin' Brig, at the south end of the Cairn o'Mounth road.

Toilets: None on route.

Charr bothy in Glen Dye

Curiously, Joseph Robertson described how, in a field near the 'highway', a lone tree marked the spot where the cottage and kailyard of a notorious warlock, Colin Massie, once stood. Massie's mother and brother lived with him in Glen Dye. Was this the same place? No one knows, but there is certainly an odd sense of desolation about it.

Keep an eye open on the high tops to the left, where red deer are often seen grazing. As you head along the track you will see a group of buildings in the distance. One of them is the Charr bothy, at the junction of the Water of Charr and the Dye. Nearer to it, not far from a pond behind a high fence, the track turns sharp right, goes uphill for a short distance, and then turns left to the bothy.

Charr bothy in Glen Dye

The bothy is bare but solidly wind- and waterproof, which is all that the majority of hill-walkers want. From the entries in the visitors' book it would seem that most people are happy enough with it – 'Great bothy for the kids', read one entry. As a plaque on the door indicates, Fasque Estates handed over the care of the building to the Mountain Bothies Association, the funding being provided by the family and friends of the late John Whitley.

This link with the MBA is interesting, for another entry dated 9 January 1993 noted that it was 'Jim Cosgrove's Birthday Party'. Jim Cosgrove, from Letham in Angus, was a veteran member of the MBA who did a one-man repair job on many bothies in the north-east. He was also a leading member of the Scottish Rights of Way Society and it was his 80th birthday that the Charr party was celebrating. Unfortunately, the bothy has had to be closed from time to time because of vandalism.

There is a kind of windbreak wall outside the front door and you can sit there in the sun, feet up, and look across to where the Water of Charr comes tumbling down from the hills. The track beside the river, going south, leads eventually to the Clatterin' Brig at the foot of the Cairn o' Mounth.

Behind the bothy the track from the Spital pushes on towards Mount Battock into wild and desolate hill-country. This is for hardier and more experienced hillwalkers. Your route is in the opposite direction, back the way you came; for a start, at any rate. Where the track turns down to the river, take another track going straight ahead, running parallel with the track from the Spital Like the old song, you will be taking the 'high road' back to your starting point, while on the way out you took the 'low road'.

Clachnaben from Glen Dye

The 'high road' gives a new perspective on Clachnaben (or Clochnaben) country. Away in the distance you can see traffic crawling up the Cairn o' Mounth, heading for Fettercairn. The land around it is bleak and bare, as the old ballad says, and the contrasting gentleness of Glen Dye underlines this. Yet in some ways it has a kind of wild beauty of its own, with the old Clach sticking its knotted head up defiantly among the surrounding hills.

The road back climbs steadily, then drops down and heads for Glendye Lodge, which is 5km from the Charr bothy. After passing a small belt of trees, about 1.5km from the lodge, it links up with another track coming up from the Water of Dye. This is the track that takes you back to Spital Burn. This route down the hill runs close to the Dye, which at times can be an angry river.

The last lap brings you back to where you first set out on the Glen Dye track after crossing the sturdy bridge over the Dye. Now you cross it a second time. Your last obstacle is the high stile below the Cairn o' Mounth road. You have come full circle – and there's honest folk at the Spital!

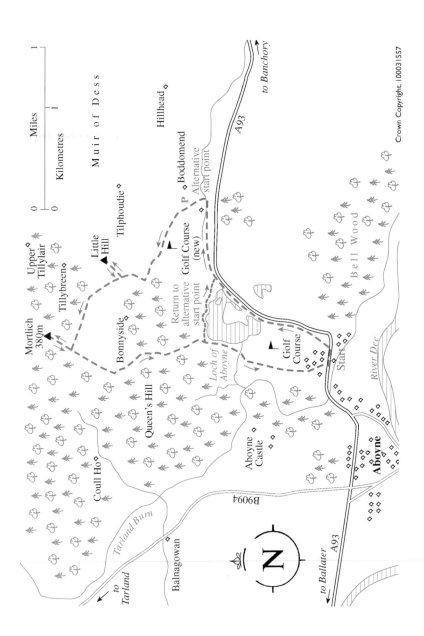

Miles

Kilometres

M u i r   o f   D e s s

Hillhead ◇

Boddomend ◇

Tilphoudie ◇

P

Alternative start point

Golf Course (new)

Upper Tillylair ◇

Little Hill ▲

Tillybreen ◇

Return to alternative start point

Mortlich 380m ▲

Bonnyside ◇

Loch of Aboyne

Golf Course

A93

to Banchory

Bell Wood

Queen's Hill

Start

River Dee

Coull Ho ◇

Aboyne Castle ◇

Aboyne

B9094

Tarland Burn

Balnagowan ◇

to Tarland

N

to Ballater

A93

Crown Copyright. 100031557

HILL OF MORTLICH

They say there is a ghost on the Hill of Mortlich above Aboyne. Back in 1900, the writer A. I. McConnochie carried a poem about him in his book, *Deeside*. He was a fearsome spectre, it said, 'clad wi' hair', with a beard that was 'three feet an mair', and he was called the Red Cap o' Mortlich.

There have been no sightings of the Red Cap for many years, but if you decide to go and look for him you are not likely to regret it. For, ghost or no ghost, a visit to this 380m hill takes you on one of the most interesting and enjoyable walks in the Aboyne area.

Start your walk along the Old Deeside Line, going in a northerly direction from a bridge beside the main A93, about 200m east from Golf Road. The line first goes beneath the bridge where the trains used to pass before going into the centre of Aboyne. The route continues between Aboyne Golf Course and the main road to Aberdeen and is pleasantly lined with mature birch trees. At Aboyne Loch Caravan Park you have some gates to negotiate, and must cross the entrance and exit to the park, but the way continues along the old track and close to Aboyne Loch. Just past the entrance road to the new 9-hole golf course, you have to cross a stile to continue along the old line, and further along, there is a second stile. By now the road has diverged away from the track and the traffic noise is less intrusive.

You soon come out onto a track next to Kirkton Cottages. Turn left here and follow the track over a cattle

INFORMATION

Distance: 9 km (5.5 miles) circular, with 260m ascent.

Start and Finish: Start on the Old Deeside railway line in Aboyne, just east from Golf Road, finish at the bottom of Golf Road on A93. For a shorter walk, park near Kirkton Cottages (signposted from A93 about 1.5 km from the centre of Aboyne), where the walk can also be finished.

Terrain: Tracks and paths, can be wet in places. Strong shoes or boots recommended. Take waterproof and windproof clothing with you.

Refreshments: Available at the 'Lodge on the Loch', on the northern shore of Aboyne Loch. Wider selection in Aboyne itself.

Toilets: In Aboyne.

Aboyne and Deeside from Little Hill

grid and keep left at the next fork. It is possible to start your walk here if you prefer a shorter route. There is a parking area on the right, and, if driving to this point you should leave the A93 where the track is signed to 'Auchinhove and Kirkton Cottages'. The route to Mortlich, however, is straight ahead, up a rough track that curves away to the left, passing a stretch of woodland. There is a small quarry on your right.

Beyond the quarry the road continues to climb steadily, opening up a magnificent view of Aboyne and its loch, with the Deeside hills in the background. Leave the track to the right, about 50m before a gate across the track. There are usually cattle in the field beyond the gate and these are best avoided, especially if you have a dog as company. A new path leads up the hill, possibly through high bracken, depending on the time of year, and is waymarked with a series of small red triangular markers, but these can be difficult to spot when the vegetation is lush.

Partway up the hill the path swings to the left, but it is worth continuing straight ahead to the top of this smaller hill, which is Little Hill. This short diversion is well worth while for the splendid views from the top, which are even better than those from the top of Mortlich because Little Hill has a very open aspect. On the summit can be found cairns; possibly from an old hill fort, and views of the Deeside hills in all directions. Having enjoyed the views, retrace your steps to the previous junction and carry on along the earlier path in a north-westerly direction. Mortlich will soon come into view.

The path reduces in width and follows a fence line on its right. The path dips somewhat and it can be wet along here for a short way. Note the small house of Tillybreen on your right; soon a fence bars the way and you need to walk a short distance to the left to cross it at a stile. Cross here and continue in the same direction as before, towards Mortlich. This path can be quite narrow, but is easy to follow, keeping a fence on your right all the way along. At the end of the field, you come to a gate on your right, turn right here and go through the gate; the path then climbs directly up the hill through woodland to the summit.

Walkers sit by the ruined monument on Mortlich Hill

The path, although indeterminate in parts, goes all the way to the top, the final push being a hard one. Small pine trees thin out as you reach the heather-clad summit. The great pile of stones on top scarcely adds to Mortlich's glory, yet at one time this modest peak – the highest point in the parish – was a conspicuous landmark in the district.

It was surmounted by a granite obelisk 20m high, topped by a metal cross. The monument was erected in 1864 to the memory of Charles, 10th Marquis of Huntly, whose ancestral home, Aboyne Castle, is about 800m north of the village. Now, all that is left of the monument is a heap of rubble. No one would know that it had ever been there unless they stumbled on the clues among the stones. One is a large piece of metal sticking up among the boulders, the remains of the cross that topped the obelisk. The other is a flat rectangular stone with a faded inscription on it. It tells how the monument was raised by the Marquis's widow, Mary Antoinette, and 'the Tenantry of Aboyne'. He died on 18th September 1863.

What happened to the monument is a bit of a mystery. On 7th November 1912, the *Aberdeen Daily Journal* reported with a faint air of surprise that the obelisk was no longer there. 'Yesterday morning', it said, 'early risers in Aboyne, on looking towards the Hill of Mortlich, were astonished to find that the monument erected on the hill in 1864 in memory of a former Marquis was gone. On investigation being made, it was found that the monument had collapsed. The wet weather and the fact that the edifice was in need of repairs were, it is said, responsible for its collapse'.

So much for lost glory. There is another piece of forgotten history buried under these stones, for a Pictish fort once stood on Mortlich's summit. A. I. McConnochie mentioned seeing the remains of a large enclosure there, but there is little sign of it now. A Pictish road could also be traced from Little Hill, on Mortlich's south-eastern slope, down to Tilphoudie and the Muir of Dess.

Whatever its history, Mortlich is a good place to take stock of Deeside. You look down over the rooftops of Aboyne, on its loch and golf course, and on the great panoramic sweep of the Dee Valley. From little Mortlich, too, you can turn full circle and nod respectfully to the big hills – Lochnagar, Morven, lumpy Clachnaben (Clochnaben), conical Mount Keen, and a few more. The way back from Mortlich is by Aboyne Loch and through the golf course to the village. Watch out for birds in the woods. Quails have been seen here, running awkwardly through the bracken and giving out their peculiar 'whit, whit, whit' call.

Return down the hill by the ascent route, but this time, when you reach the gate, continue straight on. Keep a fence and woodland on your right and follow the narrow path down and around the edge of the large field. Cross the track from Bonnyside which enters the woods and comes out on a back road linking Coull with the Tarland Road (a walk worth doing another time). Meantime, however, your way carries on along the fence line, turning left when the fence does so and walking in light woodland, still following the occasional red marker.

You soon cross a stile and still keep right, following the fence line and also a drystane dyke. Eventually the path passes through a gap in the fence beneath a large oak tree, here the path turns slightly right and you soon see the Loch of Aboyne. Follow the path down the hill towards the loch and the old golf course; when close to the loch you reach a slightly wider path.

Here you proceed according to where you started from. If you started from Kirkton Cottages, turn left here around the loch and past the Lodge on the Loch, where you may wish to stop for refreshments. Swans and ducks can often be seen feeding on the loch, which is used by Aberdeen Water Ski Club.

In past times a different kind of sport took place here – curling. Great 'bonspiels' were held, drawing competitors from far and wide. Part of the old Deeside railway line was used as a 'halt' for the curlers, and you can still see the platform where they disembarked from the train and stepped right onto the ice. Milder winters mean that the loch rarely freezes over.

Beyond the loch, follow the track until you get close to the main A93, then turn left over a stile onto the old railway line, where your route is a quieter one. Here the Deeside line has not been developed, as it has been nearer to Ballater (though there are plans to do so), but it is in reasonable condition – and maybe all the better for being a little wild. What's more, it soon leads to where your car was left, near Kirkton Cottages.

For the centre of Aboyne, cross the stile on your right, close to the loch shore, and enter the golf course. There is a clear path going through the course and walkers are allowed, though there is a warning sign to 'Keep to the Path, Keep Dogs on a Lead and Beware of Golf Balls'. Cross the course, keeping a good lookout for golfers since one of the holes crosses the path, emerge on Golf Road and it is just a short walk back to the main road close to your starting point.

Aboyne Loch

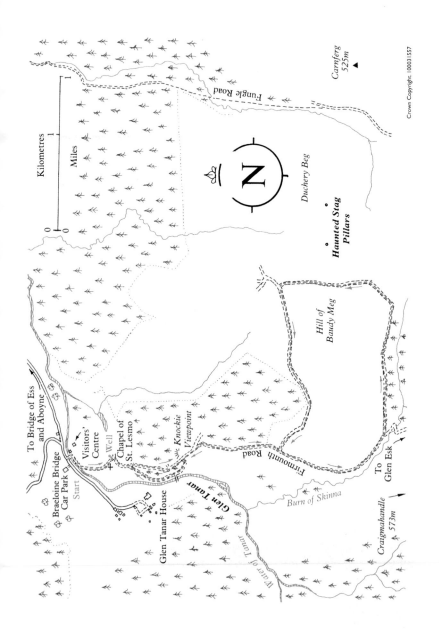

THE HAUNTED STAG

When a deer-hunting laird called Sir William Cunliffe Brooks took over the Deeside estate of Glen Tanar in 1869 he built fences to keep the deer in, not out. Trophies from the 'shoots' held in those days can still be seen in Glen Tanar House, where the ceiling of the ballroom is studded with over 500 sets of antlers and stags' heads. Under each is a tiny plaque recording the name of the hunter and the date. But one trophy is missing – the head of the Haunted Stag.

This walk takes you on the trail of the Haunted Stag, back in time to a fascinating and little-known episode in the Glen Tanar story. It starts at the Braeloine car park. Cross the old hump-back bridge on the opposite side of the road (once over, the Visitor Centre is on the left) and turn right where a huge copper beech tree guards the approach to the bridge. Waymarked routes are signposted near the bridge. Follow the red marker, which takes you along a track by the Water of Tanar. The grass on either side has been allowed to grow wild, so that in summer the start of the route is garlanded by buttercups, white and pink clover, and other wild flowers.

The track swings round towards the Chapel of St Lesmo, built by William Cunliffe Brooks in 1870, The pews of this beautiful chapel, still used to-day, are lined with deerskin. At one time antlers hung from its ceiling. The old house of Braeloine stood on the site in earlier days, the centrepiece of a busy community

INFORMATION

Distance: 10km (6 miles) circular.

Start and Finish: Braeloine Bridge car park, Glen Tanar. Take B976 from Aboyne to Bridge of Ess (about 2.5km) and follow the signs to the car park.

Terrain: Some rough walking, including uphills. Boots recommended. Take waterproofs and warm clothing.

Refreshments: None on route, take food and drink with you.

Toilets: At Braeloine Visitor Centre (if open).

Opening hours: Braeloine Visitor Centre, Glen Tanar. May - Sep open daily except Tues 10.00 -17.00. Oct - April open Thur-Mon 10.00 -17.00

Chapel of St Lesmo

known as Braeloine and Knockieside. It dated back to the early 17th century, but now there is nothing to show that it was ever there. A gate takes you through the fence to the Chapel, and an information board tells the story of Knockieside.

The graves of the old lairds lie outside the chapel. Beside the dyke around the chapel a long, high stone stands at the grave of Donald MacKintosh, Cunliffe Brooks' gamekeeper. The two men often sat at this stone while out shooting in the hills, and it was agreed that whoever died first would have it at his graveside. In May 1876, Donald was the first to go; the laird kept his promise and had the stone taken down from the hill to his keeper's burial place.

On the opposite side of the track are the remains of an old well once used by travellers going south. Beyond the chapel, the track turns right and heads up Knockie Hill through a plantation of Scots pine and larch – watch for the red waymarker. At the entrance to the woodland is another information board which says that the hill has been used by people at least since the Bronze Age, 4,500 years ago.

The climb up through the woodland is gentle, emerging at the Knockie Viewpoint. Here, an indicator board picks out the hills stretching away to the west. A rough track goes downhill towards Glen Tanar House, following the red waymarker, but your route lies straight ahead,

Keeper's stone at St Lesmo

with a lofty view of the estate on the right. Glen Tanar House can be seen through the trees, with a small loch near it where visitors can fish for trout.

The track you are following is the Firmounth Road, the old hill road from Deeside to Glenesk. On the left you will see a stone carrying the inscription 'Let Well Alone', one of many inscribed stones scattered throughout the estate (see Walk 6), while further on, near a water tank on the right, is another stone marking the site of the Monk's Well. Walking this ancient path you get some idea of the vastness of Glen Tanar Estate, and of the part afforestation has played in it. In the past it was famous for its fir, large quantities being cut and marketed for timber. The logs were floated down the Water of Tanar, and a ship named the *Countess of Aboyne* was built entirely of timber from the estate.

During the Second World War over three million cubic feet of timber was felled in Glen Tanar. Now, as you tramp along the Firmounth, you can see new plantations spreading away to the south. At one time you might also have sniffed whisky in the air, for, like many Deeside glens, illegal whisky-making was rampant here. The *Aberdeen Free Press* once reported that in the morning you could 'count the "reek" of 13 stills rising from the hillsides on the estate'.

Down in the glen, as you walk, the Tanar can be seen winding its way towards the Dee, while keeping it company is a track which runs into the hills to join the Firmounth. This is a fruitful area for bird-watchers. Redstarts and cuckoos are among the summer visitors, and you might also spot crossbills and capercaillies, which depend on Scots pine for food.

Less than a mile from the Knockie Viewpoint, a rough, stony track comes down from the Hill of Baudy Meg. Your return route will take you back to Braeloine by this track, but for the moment ignore it. Instead, head along the Firmounth track until it reaches a fork about 3 km from your starting point at Braeloine. Here, the Firmounth path drops down to the Burn of Skinna, crosses it and climbs steeply up through woodlands to the face of Craigmahandle, where it pushes its way over the hills to Glen Esk.

Notice a curiously inscribed stone beside the track before taking the left-hand fork, which eventually turns quite steeply uphill on its way to Baudy Meg. Don't get the wrong idea – there is no one called Meg waiting for you on top. The name comes from the Gaelic *badan magh*, which means the hill of hares. You may see plenty of hares on the Glen Tanar Estate, but no bawdy ladies.

Near here, on Duchery Beg, you will also see the Haunted Stag, or, at least, two stone pillars that mark the spot where it died. The track uphill is rough and stony, and a stiff push. Look away to your right and you will see Carnferg, a hill with a monument on top of it. When you are in line with this monument, you will be able to pick out the pillars in the heather. They are not far beyond a line of shooting butts and a yellow waymarker post which you pass.

William Cunliffe Brooks gave the stag its 'haunted' tag because it was a defiant animal, always escaping his gun, almost as if it was one of the mythical haunted stags that are often said to be seen in the hills. He was never able to get it in his sights long enough to bring it down. Then, on 9th October 1877, he hunted it high on Duchery Beg, where the moor stretches away to Carnferg and the old Fungle pass. Not far off the track is a pillar with a huge stone ball on top of it. This marks the spot where Cunliffe Brooks stood when he fired the fatal shot. Farther away, deep in the heather, is a similar pillar and ball. It stands 267 feet (81 m) from the first pillar – the exact distance at which Cunliffe Brooks shot his elusive stag.

In those days a 'kill' at this distance was regarded as a considerable feat, and Cunliffe Brooks, who was never known for his modesty, erected his own monument to commemorate the event; two monuments, to be exact. Faded inscriptions on the stone balls carry the words The Haunted Stag, and then declare, 'The Stag is dead. Sure bullet to its fatal mark hath sped'.

Jimmy Oswald, Glen Tanar's former head keeper, had a record of the Haunted Stag's shooting in his Game Book, but the whereabouts of the antlers is a mystery. It is thought that they might have hung with other antlers

One of the Haunted Stag stones

in St Lesmo Chapel. These were later removed when it was decided that trophies from dead deer were not the most suitable adornments for a place of worship.

Continue along the track, keeping an eye open for a track going sharply off to the left. Take this track, which runs along the side of Baudy Meg and drops down to the track you were on earlier – the Firmounth Road. The last part of the old track is stony, sandy and often slippery, so care has to be taken. Once back on the Firmounth track, retrace your steps to the Knockie Viewpoint and go downhill to the Tanar Water, near Glen Tanar House. Turn right, and go through a gate straight ahead of you.

About 100 metres beyond the gate, go left on the red route, which follows an attractive path by the riverside back to Braeloine and the car park.

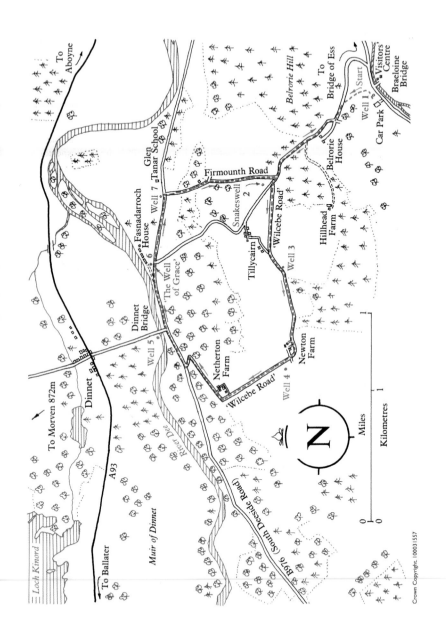

WILCEBE ROAD

The name 'Wilcebe Road' has never appeared in any map or guidebook. The road is on Belrorie Hill, in Glen Tanar Estate, and was coined from the initials of an eccentric 19th century laird, William Cunliffe Brooks. Will C. Brooks... Will C.B... Wilcebe. The initials WCB can be seen on wells, seats, walls and stones all over the estate, along with cryptic homilies to passers-by. One near the entrance to the glen warns 'Beware of the Deer' while another reads 'Honest water never left man in the mire'.

In the vicinity of Wilcebe Road there are no fewer than seven wells, each carrying a message from the laird, some blunt, some humorous, some inexplicable. To-gether, they lead you into a delightful corner of Glen Tanar, well away from the main visitor areas.

The first well is at the car park, where there is a water-trough opposite Braeloine Bridge. It carries the Gaelic inscription *Ceud Mile Failte*, wishing you 'A Hundred Thousand Welcomes'. Go through a gate behind the well and cross the car park track to a narrow path with a sign pointing to 'Juniper Trail'. Further up the path, another sign points rightward to a viewpoint, which looks down on the glen.

Back on the path, go through a small gate and into a field where hill ponies some-times graze. This leads to yet another gate, which opens onto a tarmac road running from Glen Tanar to the B976. It takes you past Belrorie House, where a giant sequoia tree towers up on the right of the road.

The road passes a track to Hillhead Farm, and as you go downhill a superb view of the Dee Valley opens up on your right. Mighty Morven can be seen, and little Mullach Hill, crowned with Mullach's Cairn, traditionally marking the spot where a Danish king is said to have fallen; then there is Loch Kinord on the Muir of Dinnet, and in the distance the long ridge of Pressendye behind Tarland.

INFORMATION

Distance: 6.5km (4 miles) circular.

Start and Finish: Braeloine Bridge car park, Glen Tanar. Take B976 from Aboyne to Bridge of Ess (about 2.5km) and follow the signs to the car park.

Terrain: Road or good tracks all the way. No special footwear needed.

Refreshments: None on route. Take food and drink with you.

Toilets: At Braeloine Visitor Centre (if open).

Opening hours: Braeloine Visitor Centre, Glen Tanar. May - Sep open daily except Tues 10.00 - 17.00. Oct - April open Thur-Mon 10.00 -17.00

One of the Wilcebe Road wells

At a fork, a track leads off to the right. At the top of it you will see a huge rectangular stone, a granite memorial erected by the indefatigable Cunliffe Brooks. It carries the barely readable inscription 'Fir Munth. Ancient Pass over the Grampians. Here crossed the invading armies of Edward I of England AD 1296 and 1303. Also the army of Montrose 1645'. Some experts say the laird was wrong on all three counts! This track is your return route.

At the next fork, 50m ahead, you will see the second well – Snakeswell. It got the name because its inscription read: 'The worm of the still is the deadliest snake on the hill', an obvious allusion to the illicit whisky distilling that went on around here. A semi-circular wall shelters it, with some of the stones acting as a seat for thirsty wayfarers.

At the fork, on a stone in the wall on the left, is the sign 'Wilcebe Road'. Follow it to the left, passing Tillycairn Farm, and where the road bends right, set well back on the left and partly overgrown, is the third well. Unlike some of the other wells, this one is still giving out water. There is even a drinking cup attached to it. Take heed of what WCB had to say about it. The inscription on the well reads 'Well to know when you are Well off'.

The road turns right at Newton Farm (about 1.3 km from the Wilcebe Road sign), and heads north-west. Watch for the entrance to a field on your left, set well back from the road and with a curious pile of twisted stones on the left-hand side of the gate. These are the kind of grotesque stones that Cunliffe Brooks used in different parts of the estate – you will see some on the dykes in Wilcebe Road.

The stones have been built around the fourth well, which has no running water. Its cryptic message reads 'Drink, Thank, Think'. What our eccentric laird expected us to think about will never be known, but perhaps it was the land around his wells, rich and fertile, stretching away to the Dee and the distant hills.

The road now goes down to Netherton Farm, where it turns right; at the corner two more giant sequoia trees stand guard on either side of the track. On the wall around one of the trees is that familiar sign – 'Wilcebe Road'.

But soon you leave Wilcebe Road. Go sharp left down to the B976 and turn right along it. Two mysterious wells lie ahead. The fifth is at Dinnet Bridge, but is almost inaccessible. It can be seen on the west (Dinnet) side of the river, at the foot of the nearest side of the bridge as you approach it. It is difficult to imagine why anyone should build a well only a few feet from the river. Even more inexplicable is the inscription – 'Alike yet so different'.

The next well, the sixth, is built into the dyke at Fasnadarroch House, about 500m from the bridge on your way towards Aboyne. Look for it on your left. The inscription says: 'The Well of Grace'. What romantic story lies behind that simple phrase?

A mare and its foal on the path to Wilcebe Road

The seventh and last well is the Daddy of them all – the most unusual, and some say the most unsightly. It was built into the wall of the old Glen Tanar School to celebrate the Jubilee of Queen Victoria, 'a bright and shining light to her people'. The well carries a number of Cunliffe Brooks' inscriptions. One seems to be directed at square pegs in round holes. 'Shape thyself for use', it reads, 'the stone that may fit in the wall is not left in thy way'.

Across the road from the well is the Firmounth track, which is signposted. Follow it past the cottage called Gean Brae and turn off on a track on the right. This is the track that leads to the Edward I stone, and from there down Belrorie Hill to the car park. You are back where you started – at the end of the Seven Wells walk.

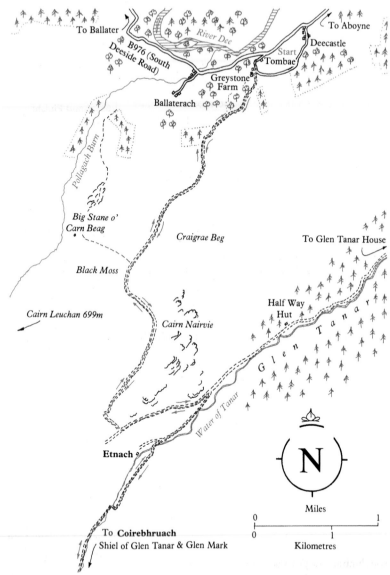

To Ballater

B976 (South Deeside Road)

River Dee

To Aboyne

Deecastle

Start

Tombae

Greystone Farm

Ballaterach

Pollagach Burn

Big Stane o' Carn Beag

Craigrae Beg

To Glen Tanar House

Black Moss

Half Way Hut

Cairn Leuchan 699m

Cairn Nairvie

Glen Tanar

Water of Tanar

Etnach

N

Miles

0   1

0   1

To **Coirebhruach**
Shiel of Glen Tanar & Glen Mark

Kilometres

Crown Copyright. 100031557

ETNACH AND COIREBHRUACH

We'll up the moor of Charlestown
And o'er the water of Dee,
And hine away to Candecaill,
It's there that we should be.

That verse from an old song points the way to what was once one of the most important Mounth passes from Deeside to the south; it went, according to a 17th century list of routes, from the River Dee to the River Tay, 'from Canakyle to Innermarkie'. Innermarkie was Invermark in Glen Esk, Charlestown was Aboyne, and Candecaill or Canakyle was what is now known as Deecastle, 6km east of Ballater on the South Deeside Road (B976).

The name Canakyle has changed over the years, but the correct version is believed to be Ceann-na-Coille, meaning Woodhead or Woodend. It was here on the south side of the Dee that the first Marquis of Huntly built Dee Castle, which became the principal residence of his family, but it was accidentally burned to the ground in 1641. Some years later it was replaced by a shooting lodge.

Although the Mounth road has long since slipped into disuse, you can still follow this ancient route through the Glentanar hills to Mount Keen and Glenesk. The starting point is Tombae, a little west of Deecastle. From here the road goes up past the farm of Greystone, whose farmhouse is built in the distinctive style introduced by Sir William Cunliffe Brooks when he was laird of Glen Tanar. Some people complained that he was bringing an English oast-house style to Scotland.

The rough track from Greystone clears the woods and pushes up the west side of Craigrae Beg. It is a long, steady climb, but not too demanding. On the right as you climb are the peaty acres of the Black Moss, stretching away to Cairn Leuchan. Here and there, grouse come squawking out of the heather. The Institute of Terrestrial Ecology at Banchory carried out grouse research on these moors. On the brow of the hill the way is barred by a gate and fence. On the other side, as a stone-mounted information panel indicates, you are in the National Nature Reserve of Glen Tanar.

INFORMATION

Distance: 11km (7 miles) to Etnach and back. Add a further 5km (3 miles) for Coirebhruach.

Start and Finish: Tombae, about halfway between Aboyne and Ballater on B976. Park in unofficial layby a few hundred metres west of Tombae (towards Ballater).

Terrain: Good tracks all the way, no steep climbs. Boots or strong shoes recommended. Take waterproof and windproof clothing.

Refreshments: None on route. Take food and drink with you. Wide choice in Aboyne ro Ballater.

Toilets: None on route.

Looking down on Etnach from the hill above the farm

Etnach from the main Glen
Tanar road to Mount Keen

The track here becomes rougher as it swings round Cairn
Nairvie (the name means 'hill of the dyke'), finally heading downhill towards the Water of Tanar. Ahead, the
green grass of Etnach begins to appear. The track turns
left where a line of shooting butts crosses the heather,
heading down to the Glen Tanar track. Some outbuildings come into view on the higher slopes of Etnach, then
the old keeper's house can be seen nestling on the edge
of the Tanar. Behind it, river and road chase each other
uphill towards Coirebhruach at the head of the glen.

The ghost of Queen Victoria will keep you company
here. This was the route she took when returning to
Balmoral from one of her Great Expeditions. 'Eatnoch',
was how she entered it in her diary. When the Queen
was there in 1861 the only person to be seen was 'a
wretched idiot girl', who sat on the ground 'with her
hands round her knees, rocking herself to and fro and
laughing'. She was blissfully unaware that she was in
the presence of royalty.

It is hard to believe that great bellowing herds of cattle
once stirred the dust on this remote pass from Deecastle
to Etnach – 'a lonely place', Queen Victoria called it –
and even today, with hill-walkers tramping through Glen
Tanar, it still seems isolated from the outside world.
This was the way the drovers came in their long trek to
the trysts in the south, down from Strathdon and
Gairnside, over the Dee and 'hine away to Candecaill'.
They halted at Etnach for the night before pushing on
to Coirebhruach at the head of Glen Tanar.

Etnach is about 8km from Glen Tanar House. Walkers
deciding to skip the return journey to Greystone can

arrange to be picked up at the car park near the estate buildings. But your route lies in the opposite direction, turning right at Etnach, past a sturdy stone bridge spanning the Tanar and on to Coirebhruach. This was another drovers' stop, for in the days of the great cattle drives there was an inn here, serving thirsty travellers making the giant 'leap-frog' over Mount Keen to Glenmark. A rickle of stones is all that remains of the inn.

A few hundred yards from Coirebhruach, up the Tanar, is the site of the Shiel of Glentanar, once a shooting lodge, where many a weary traveller found shelter when the winds came howling off Mount Keen. At one time there was a graffiti scribble on a wall saying that one George Sutherland had stabled his horse there in 1890. He was back in 1922, 'enjoying a picnic', but this time he came by car.

Coirebhruach is the turn-around point on this walk, taking you back by Etnach to Tombae. On the way there, look for two fading tracks just past the gate at the Glen Tanar boundary. The second track goes off to the Pollogach Burn, where the Ordnance Survey map shows a rocking stone on the east bank.

Henry Alexander, later Sir Henry, Lord Provost of Aberdeen and author of the classic book *The Cairngorms*, saw the same map entry back in the 1920s and went in search of the rocking stone. It was first recorded by the Ordnance Survey in 1865 and was known locally as the Big Stone of Cam Beag. Nowadays, it is impossible to get even the slightest movement out of it. Perhaps young Geordie Byron did better. It was up by the Pollogach Burn that the young poet came when he spent his holidays at Ballaterach, wandering across the grey-brown moors and looking across the Dee to the 'dark Lochnagar' that he was later to write about so memorably.

Ballaterach is only a short distance from Greystone Farm. Isaac Stephen, a carpenter, had a workshop at Greystone and the young Byron was always nosing about the place. He was, said Isaac, 'an ill-tricket nickum' – a mischievous lad. Isaac's daughter, Mrs Calder, who was married to the farmer at Greystone, described Byron as 'a very takkin laddie, but nae easily managed'.

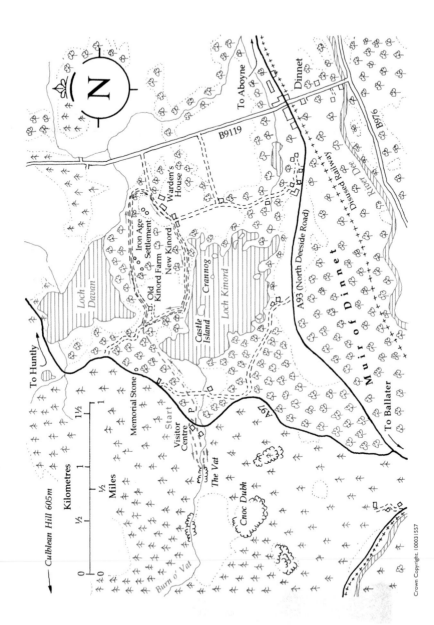

To Aboyne

Dinnet

B9119

B976

River Dee

A93 (North Deeside Road)

Disused Railway

Warden's House

Iron Age Settlement

New Kinord

Old Kinord Farm

Crannog

Loch Kinord

Loch Davan

Castle Island

Muir of Dinnet

To Huntly

Memorial Stone

Start

Visitor Centre

P

The Vat

A97

Cnoc Dubh

To Ballater

Burn o' Vat

Culblean Hill 605m

Kilometres

Miles

0 ½ 1 1½

0 ½ 1

N

Crown Copyright. I 00031557

MUIR OF DINNET

The Muir of Dinnet is a National Nature Reserve covering 1520 hectares of undulating heath, glorious with purple heather in late summer, and crowned by the twin lochs of Kinord and Davan. Culblean Hill slopes down to the western shores of the two lochs. From it a turbulent burn feeds Loch Kinord after passing through one of Deeside's most spectacular attractions – the Vat.

Burn o' Vat is the starting point for a two-in-one walk which includes the Vat and takes you on a circular tour of the Muir. Before setting off, it is worth calling in at the Visitor Centre to find out more about the area. There is information on the vast range of wildlife (everything from microscopic water creatures to red deer and including 150 different kinds of birds and over 400 moths).

The first part of the walk starts at a sign, 'The Vat', on the edge of a wood behind the Centre. Follow the sign and go through the wood to the Vat Burn, which is crossed by a bridge. Once over the bridge, the route climbs up a lovely little glen where orchids can be seen in summer. It passes a wooden bridge on the right and comes to a dead-end at what seems to be an impenetrable rock barrier. Here you will see the burn tumbling through a narrow gap in the rocks – the entrance to the Vat.

To enter it you have to clamber over large rocks and pick your way up the burn over stones leading to the entrance. Take care – one slip and you will get your feet wet! Inside the Vat you will find yourself in a huge bowl-like cavern. Ringed with high rock and narrowly open

INFORMATION

Distance: Burn o'Vat walk, 4km (2.5 miles) circular. Walkway section, 1.5km (1 mile). Total for two loops, 5.5km (3.5 miles).

Start and finish: Burn o'Vat car park. Take A93 and between Aboyne and Ballater, turn off on B9119 (signed to Strathdon). Burn o'Vat is reached in about 2km.

Terrain: **Easy** walking on good tracks and paths. Boots or wellies needed if you go into the Vat.

Refrshments: None on route. Wide choice in Aboyne or Ballater.

Opening hours: The Visitor Centre is normally open daily, Easter to September.

Burn o' Vat

to the sky, this giant pothole was formed after the last Ice Age. The burn running into it pours through a spectacular gorge between Cnoc Dubh and Culblean Hill.

It is an impressive sight. The Vat itself must have sheltered many a fugitive, but the most famous was a freebooter called Gilderoy MacGregor, who is said to have hidden behind a waterfall with just enough room to hold a man. Gilderoy was captured and hanged in 1658.

When you leave the Vat, go down the path, turn left over the bridge and climb the stone steps, turning right at the top to reach the special viewpoint which looks across Loch Kinord. The walkway ends at the car park where you started.

For the second stage of the walk, leave the car park and cross the road to where a marker post can be seen in the heather. There are red arrows to show you the way. Follow them till you come to a small parking area where there is a cairn with a map of the Nature Reserve. Above it is a plaque commemorating the Queen's Silver Jubilee in 1977. From here the red arrows take you deeper into the wood. Follow them until you come to a post showing both a red and a green arrow. The red arrow is part of the return route, so ignore it until later. The green arrow takes you up a brae to all that remains of old Kinord Farm.

Away to the left, hidden by the trees, is Loch Davan. Less accessible than Loch Kinord, it is rich in bird life. As many as 24,000 wintering geese have been seen on Davan, as well as mute and whooper swans. Stand on the road at the head of the loch as dusk falls on an October evening and you can watch the breathtaking spectacle of thousands of geese coming in to land.

Beyond the ruins of Old Kinord Farm, a red gate leads into an attractive birchwood. Most of the trees are little more than 30 years old: one of the most important developments at the Reserve has been the recolonisation of birch.

The track, well marked by green arrows, leads to a road approaching the Reserve from Dinnet, but before reaching the road, watch out on the left for some circular enclosures that look like monster stone circles. These are the remains of an Iron Age settlement, one of three prehistoric sites going back 2500-3000 years.

Leaving the settlement, continue on the track until it reaches the road from Dinnet. Turn right, past the ranger's house and out into the open ground above Loch Kinord. In early summer, rafts of white water lily and the rarer yellow lily lie on the surface.

Fishing on Loch Kinord

There were three lochs on the Muir of Dinnet in prehistoric times, but one silted up and turned into a peat bog, which is still there today. Fishing is allowed on Loch Kinord, but only for pike, perch and eel. The favourite spot for fishing – and picnicking – is further up the loch.

Along the main path you will come to a green arrow pointing to a path going down to the edge of the loch. It takes you along the lochside. Not far offshore you will see a man-made island or 'crannog', built about 2,000 years ago. Long after these lake-dwellers had vanished, another island a little to the west – Castle Island – was turned into a medieval fortress. Malcolm Canmore, King of Scotland from 1058 to 1093, had a hunting lodge on it and Edward I is thought to have stayed there while his army camped on the moor. James IV spent a couple of nights in the castle in 1504.

It was said at one time that there had been eleven spellings of the name Kinord, and one of them was Canmore. Others included Kender, Ceander, Ceanmore and Kinnord. Another green arrow shows you where the lochside path turns up to the main track and to one final link with the past – a Pictish symbol stone, nearly two metres high and probably dating from the 9th century. It is fenced in and stands a little way above the loch, hidden by broom.

Not far from the Pictish stone, the track turns away from the loch, heading along a field on the right towards Davan. This leads to the junction below Old Kinord Farm, where you first saw both red and green arrows. The red arrows will now take you back over the new path to the B119 and the Burn o' Vat car park.

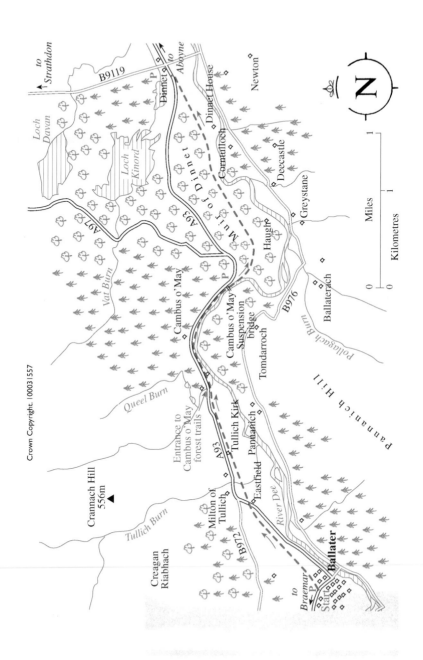

Crown Copyright 10003 1557

THE DEESIDE RAILWAY

A century and more ago, directors of the Great North of Scotland Railway Company held weekend board meetings in a saloon coach shunted into a siding at Cambus o' May station, near Ballater, when they had business to discuss. They knew what they were doing, for as they sat there talking about railway matters, and wining and dining in style, they found themselves looking out on one of the loveliest views on Deeside.

In those days, many people travelled from Aberdeen to Cambus o' May by train to picnic on the banks of the River Dee. The railway closed in 1966 and the trippers now travel by car, but the old Royal line carries a different kind of traffic – walkers with packs on their backs. The railway line is being developed as a long distance walk, right from Duthie Park in Aberdeen to Ballater. The stretch from Ballater to Dinnet is particularly attractive, offering excellent views of Deeside.

Your walk starts in the station square in Ballater, but first take a little time to see the exhibition of the Victorian royal railway carriage and of Queen Victoria's arrival at the station. As a plaque on the station wall says, Ballater Station was for over a century the scene of Royal arrivals and departures through six reigns from Queen Victoria in her 'Palace on Wheels' to Queen Elizabeth II. The plaque commemorates the rebuilding of the station in 1886, when a Royal Waiting Room was opened for Queen Victoria's use. The Royal loo is still there!

INFORMATION

Distance: 10km (6 miles) one way.

Start: Ballater Station.

Finish: Dinnet, on the A93, 10km east of Ballater (you can return by bus).

Terrain: Easy walking on a good path. No special footwear needed.

Refreshments: Tearoom at Ballater Station, plus wide choice in Ballater itself. Tearoom at Dinnet. Picnic site at Cambus o'May.

Toilets: Church Square, Ballater.

Opening hours: Tourist Information Centre, Station Square, Ballater, open all year, summer 0900-1800, winter 1000-1700 daily. Includes an exhibition on the old railway line.

Cambus o' May
suspension bridge

Go through to the old platform and turn right along the route of the line. There are map boards and fingerposts to show the way. Also at the start of the walk are some carved wooden posts with illustrated metal plaques which form part of the Patrick Geddes Way. Take a moment to look at the signs which celebrate the life of this Ballater-born 'Father of Town Planning'.

The route passes through a housing estate where signs indicate 'Ballater to Cambus o'May Walkway', though there's little chance of getting lost on this route. The village is soon left behind and there's pleasant walking along Deeside. From the walkway, look behind you to see the outline of the Coyles of Muick in the distance, and behind them is the great bulk of Lochnagar – a magnificent backcloth to the Royal Deeside town.

The route continues adjacent to Monaltrie Park with good views of the 'pudding bowl' shape of Craigendarroch on the left. You then reach Eastfield on the A93 where the old rail bridge has been removed and it is necessary to drop down and cross the main road; care is needed here as fast-moving traffic presents a real hazard. Continue to cross the wooden bridge over the Burn of Tullich, which comes tumbling down from Byron's 'Morven of the Snows'.

Tullich kirkyard

Just beyond the Tullich Burn you reach the ruined Kirk of Tullich, which is little more than a stone's throw from the walkway. It is an ancient and fascinating place, with a picturesque circular wall and a valuable collection of Pictish sculptured stones. Tullich was a busy little hamlet at one time, with its own market cross, but when Pannanich blossomed and a new bridge was built over the Dee at Ballater, the community died. The famous Reel of Tullich is said to have originated there when kirk-goers were stamping their feet against the cold while waiting for their minister to turn up.

A short way beyond the old kirk, a granite obelisk stands atop a birch-clad knoll on your right. The monument, which can best be seen as you approach the knoll, was raised in memory of William Farquharson of Monaltrie, whose Uncle Francis fought at the head of the Farquharsons at the Battle of Culloden in 1746. It was Francis who built an inn and developed Pannanich as a spa after 'miracle' waters were discovered there in 1760.

Pannanich, with its water, and Tullich, with its ancient kirkyard, glower at each other across the valley as if remembering the days when they competed for the crowds who came to Deeside for 'the cure'. If the cure didn't work, Tullich usually claimed the losers. The present Pannanich Wells Hotel can be seen across the Dee under Pannanich Hill. They still sell Pannanich water there, but no one now claims that it has miraculous properties.

Beyond the monument there is an opportunity to leave the old railway line, cross the main road and visit the Cambus o' May forest trails. These offer short walks around beautiful woods with several interesting geological features which are well described on interpretive boards. Return to the railway line to continue towards the Cambus o' May suspension bridge. As you walk, you can see the Dee curving round towards Cambus, a reminder of the meaning of the name – Cambus o' May, *camas mhaigh*, the Bend of the Plain. Some old spellings have it as Camas or Camus.

The route is lined with birch trees forming a silver guard of honour on either side. Wild roses bloom and, come

June, the broom bursts out in all its golden splendour. Our path kinks towards the river, just before reaching the next house. Once a wayside inn, this was known as Cutaway Cottage. When the railway came to Ballater, it was so close to the line that one corner of it had to be cut off to allow the trains to pass. Curiously enough, it worked, but it must have rattled the crockery every time the 3.30 to Ballater went up the line.

Soon you see the long white span of the Cambus o'May Bridge. This was where the day trippers from Aberdeen swam and picnicked, and still do, below the bridge, which looks as good as it did when it was built in 1905. In fact, this bridge is a replacement built in 1984, but it looks exactly like the original. When the old bridge was found to be badly in need of repair it was felt that it would be better to build a new one, so the replacement went up at a cost of £80,000. It was opened by the late Queen Mother in September 1988.

Just beyond the bridge is the old railway platform, where the former station building has now become Cambus Cottage. It has been turned into an attractive home, with an enviable view from the kitchen window. Walkers are kept away from it and a small car park has been laid out just off the main road, giving access down to the river by a set of steps.

But our route continues eastwards through a wooded area consisting of birch and pine. Look out for the signs of the old railway, there are typical fence posts and gates which once acted as crossing points over the line. There are also many old sleepers piled close to the line from the time when the track was lifted after the railway ceased to operate.

The line now passes through the Muir of Dinnet, once an open area of heather but increasingly invaded by regenerating birch trees. Along this stretch of the path the River Dee comes very close on the right and good views are possible. You cross a track which leads down to Dinnet House. Keep walking and soon you will come towards the centre of the village of Dinnet. Here you can visit the Loch Kinord Hotel or the Victoria Tearooms for refreshments while you wait for one of the regular buses to return you along Deeside, back to Ballater.

Cambus o' May station

Plans were made at one time to carry the line on from Ballater to Braemar, but Queen Victoria did not approve the idea. Now the whole Royal line has gone and all that is left is a walkway where people can stroll in peace and enjoy the magnificent scenery.

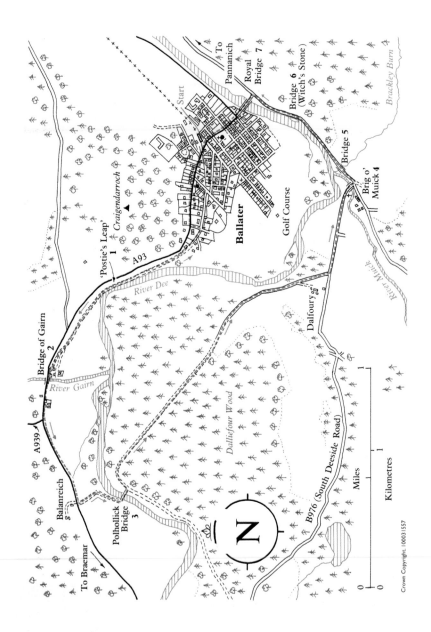

THE SEVEN BRIGS

Some lovely wooded countryside is the setting for the Seven Brigs Walk. It takes in three rivers and a handful of burns and it starts by walking from Station Square along the Braemar Road and crossing over onto the left (south) side of the road. At the Auld Kirk Hotel, turn left along Invercauld Road where a fingerpost indicates the route for the Seven Bridges Walk.

Take the next on the right, Dundarroch Road. Here you will see the first of the waymarkers, painted with a blue band, which are followed along our route. You are now on the line of the old railway track built to go beyond Ballater towards Braemar, but never completed, and now a favourite walk with both locals and visitors.

The Auld Line runs for about 1.5 km from the old station to the Fit of Gairn. The path runs parallel to the River Dee, passing through a small woodland. At one point the river bank steepens sharply, giving a nasty drop from the path, and as a safety measure a fence has been provided.

There is romance, and a tragic ending associated with the first of the Seven Brigs. You will see a bridge spanning a wide ravine known as the 'Postie's Leap'. Local legend relates that when a lovelorn postman was jilted on the eve of his wedding, he walked along the Auld Line and jumped to his death from this, the first of the Seven Brigs. A sad tale indeed.

Continuing on along this delightful stretch of the old track you reach the end of the line at Fit of Gairn. There have been three bridges over the Gairn, the first being a pack-bridge only a few feet wide. The second was built at the end of the 18th century, and the present bridge was erected in 1855. 'Not nearly as romantic looking as the old bridge' wrote a local minister, the Rev James Crombie, and he was right.

Cross the Gairn, our second bridge, and carefully cross the road – traffic can be quite fast along this stretch. Once safely across, look for the waymarkers indicating the way up a steep bank and onto a narrow path

INFORMATION

Distance: 7km (4.5 miles) circular.

Start and Finish: Station Square, Ballater. Free parking in Station Square and Church Square.

Terrain: Roads and good tracks. No special footwear needed.

Refreshments: Wide choice in Ballater.

Toilets: Church Square, Ballater.

Opening hours: Tourist Information Centre, Station Square, Ballater, open all year round, summer 0900 to 1800, winter 1000 to 1700 daily.

Polhollick Bridge

which parallels the road, but safely away from it. This path is followed until it drops to cross the road up to Strathdon and Tomintoul, then climbs again to continue westwards.

Eventually the path drops down again and our route again crosses the main Deeside Road. Opposite the farm of Balanreich a track goes down towards the Dee; follow this to reach number three, the Polhollick Bridge, which is a long white suspension bridge, built in 1892 with money provided by a Ballater exile, Alexander Gordon from Kent, who also paid for the Cambus o'May bridge.

Before the bridge was erected there was a ferry at Polhollick, crossing a well-known angling pool known as the Boat Pool. The boathouse is still in use today as a dwelling. There is a wooden hut on the west side of the river, close to the bridge. This is a river monitoring station, with sensors which detect the height of the river and also the flow rate, and is one of a number along the length of the Dee.

It is now about 3km to our next bridge, the Brig o'Muick. The route goes through Daliefour Wood, a great pinewood which hugs the Dee in both directions. Look towards Ballater, through the trees and across the Dee to see the golf course and the plum pudding hill of Craigendarroch, the 'crag of the oaks'. The track continues through the wood until it reaches the B976, where we turn left towards Ballater.

Pass Dalfoury, where John Mitchell lived. He was a skilled angler and a well-known poacher. He is said to have written a book in which he described how he was a bachelor for 40 years, married for 26 years, widowed for three years and married again for 55 years. In the book was a poem with the lines:

> *Between my cradle and my grave, I wean*
> *Seven monarchs and a queen have been*

Just before we reach the Brig o'Muick, enter the graveyard on your right. This is Glenmuick Kirkyard, where faded tombstones tell of the people who lived in this corner of Deeside a century or more ago. Near the gate you will see a coffin-shaped slab which is the grave of John Mitchell. The dates on it, which are now very difficult to read, say 1596 to 1722, a life of 126 years.

Now cross the Bridge of Muick, built in 1858 and on your right, just past the road down Glen Muick, is the Victoria memorial and seat. A large plaque here commemorates one of Queen Victoria's last public acts – taking the salute at a march past of Gordon Highlanders shortly before they set off for the Boer War in 1899. The queen was by then getting frail, and she died in 1901, having reigned for 64 years.

Plaque at Bridge of Muick

Our way carries on to reach bridge number five, the bridge over the Brackley Burn, before it meets the Dee. Beyond the bridge are two houses, Burnfoot and Bridgefoot. Carry on along the B976 and the road starts to climb; towards the highest point is a very insignificant bridge, our sixth, built with a parapet just on the one side. The high point in the road is known as Spinnin' Jenny's. Jenny was a witch. A rock which once stood at the roadside near here was known as Spinnin' Jenny's Stane, or the Witch's Stone.

Once past this bridge it isn't far until you turn left towards Ballater and reach our seventh and last bridge over the Dee. Ballater has had three bridges on or near this site. The first was a stone bridge built about 100m east of the present bridge in 1783. It was swept away by floods in 1799 and a second stone bridge was built in 1809. The floods came again – the Muckle Spate of 1829 – and away went another bridge. When the first two arches collapsed, the splash of the water was so great that it rose over the tops of nearby houses. One half-drowned visitor who had come to Pannanich for its health-giving water said wryly, 'Call you this a watering-place?'

Next came a wooden bridge. That was in 1834 and it lasted until November 1885, when the present bridge was opened by Queen Victoria, who named it the Royal Bridge. Look over the east parapet wall and you will see the foundations of the 1834 timber bridge running in a line across the river.

Across the river you enter Ballater and it is just a short walk back past the shops to reach the Station Square. For a peaceful picnic at the end of your walk, go down Golf Road to the golf course where there is a riverside footpath and lovely picnic spot.

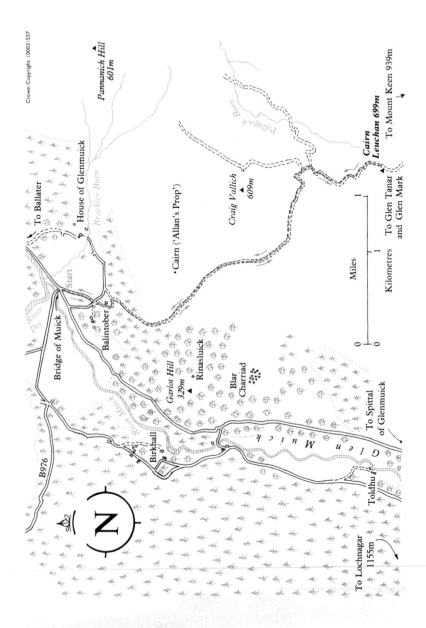

Crown Copyright: 10003155 7

CAIRN LEUCHAN

The dusty tracks across the hills of Deeside were once vital links between busy communities. They went over the Mounth from Aboyne to Tarfside, from Braemar to Braedownie, from Glen Muick to Glen Clova. One of the most important routes was the Whisky Road, starting near Ballater and crossing the moors to Glen Tanar and Glen Mark.

To follow this old whisky trail, make your way to the Bridge of Muick, about 1.5 km from Ballater on the South Deeside Road (B976). Here you will see a memorial marking the spot where Queen Victoria took the salute as the Gordon Highlanders marched off to the Boer War. To the left is a track with a sign marked 'Balintober'. This takes you up to the keeper's house at Balintober, to the right of the House of Glenmuick. Just beyond Balintober the road swings left and right and climbs uphill to a deer fence. Go through the gate and you are on the edge of a vast expanse of moorland.

Below on the right is Glen Muick, and if you look hard enough as you make your way up the hill you will see an indistinct path coming up through the heather. It is a link with a 'lost' community, a scattering of ruined settlements hidden away from the cars that stream up the Glen Muick road on their way to the Spittal and the

INFORMATION

Distance: 10km (6 miles) circular.

Start and Finish: Bridge of Muick, 1.5km from Ballater on B976. Limited parking at start: alternatively, walk from Ballater or arrange to be dropped off.

Terrain: Good tracks all the way, steady climb to Cairn Leuchan. Boots or strong shoes recommended. Take waterproof and warm clothing.

Refreshments: Wide choice in Ballater. None on route, take food and drink with you.

Toilets: In Ballater.

On top of Cairn Leuchan

hills of Lochnagar. These settlements were scattered throughout the glen from Bridgend to the Spittal, or Spittelhauche as it was called in 1600. They had names like Bog, Rinasluick, Balnoe, Byallachur, Toildow or Toldhu (the black hole), and Clashmuick (the pigs' furrow). On Garlot Hill, which you can see from the Balintober road, you can still pick out the lines of run-rig farming.

Perhaps the most interesting site is Blar Charriad. It was shown on an 1869 map as Balacariag, and was said to be 'a substantial township of twelve houses, three enclosures and a corn-drying kiln'. The kiln is still there, and you feel as if you were walking through a recognisable township. It was linked to another settlement shown on the 1869 map as Loinmore, where there were five houses. The map also shows a track running across the moor from Loinmore to the hill road from Balintober – the road you are walking on. The heather has almost buried this link with the ruined settlements, but at one time there was a steady movement of people and cattle going south over the hills.

The name Blar Charriad means 'field of conflicts'. It may be that one of the conflicts involved John Farquharson of Inverey, the Black Colonel, who featured in the ballad, *The Baron of Braickley*. Farquharson slew John Gordon of Brackley in a 'battle' that took place in these hills. Braichlie or Braikley House stood on the site of the present House of Glenmuick.

As you go up the hill towards the Pollogach Burn – the Pollach road, it was called – a prominent cairn can be seen on the left. This is known as Allan's Prop (a prop is a landmark), named after a previous owner of the estate, Sir Allan Mackenzie. Beyond the cairn is Craig Vallich, where the road swings left and goes on up to the ridge. It is a long, steady slog to the top, but take it easy and look about you – the views are outstanding. Three paths meet on the ridge. One goes to Pannanich Hill, the other crosses the Pollogach Moss to Glen Tanar. A sign points the way to Mount Keen. Queen Victoria wrote about riding over this sodden peat moss, adding, 'We avoided getting into any of the bogs'. Sensible woman that she was, she stayed on her pony while crossing what she called this 'soft bit'.

Your way is by the third path on the right. It climbs up
to a rock formation called Cairn Leuchan, which from
below, silhouetted against the sky, looks like some mysterious fairy castle. The track passes through a line of
grouse butts as it approaches the summit. The climb to
the top is well worth the effort. You look down into the
valley of the Muick, with the Birkhall road winding its
way towards Lochnagar. You can see the path that clears
the woods at Allt-na-guibhsaich and rises steeply towards the 'frowning glories' of Byron's mountain.

Turning round, you look into the face of Mount Keen,
the old Mounth track a hairline mark against its great
cone. The track goes over the west shoulder of the hill
some 180m below the summit. At 938m (3077ft), this
is the most easterly Munro in Scotland, and it domi-
nates the Dee valley. Up there, mountain hares flee at
your coming, their brown summer coats changing to
winter white late in the season, and hawks hover over-
head, preparing to dive on their unsuspecting prey. Deer
can be seen watching warily from a long way off.

Clouds over the Deeside hills

Cairn Leuchan is the turning-point of the walk, but it is
worth going further along the track so that you can drink
in the scenery down in Glen Muick. There are other
tracks that take you down into the glen, but car arrangements would have to be made if you were planning to do
this. So it's back by the 'fairy castle' and down to
Balintober. Before you leave Cairn Leuchan, look away to
the north-east and you will see two lochs in the distance.
These are Loch Kinord and Loch Davan, whose waters
lie like giant dewdrops on the Muir of Dinnet.

There is a wonderful sense of peace and isolation in the
moors between Glen Muick and Glen Tanar. It will
leave you wanting more.

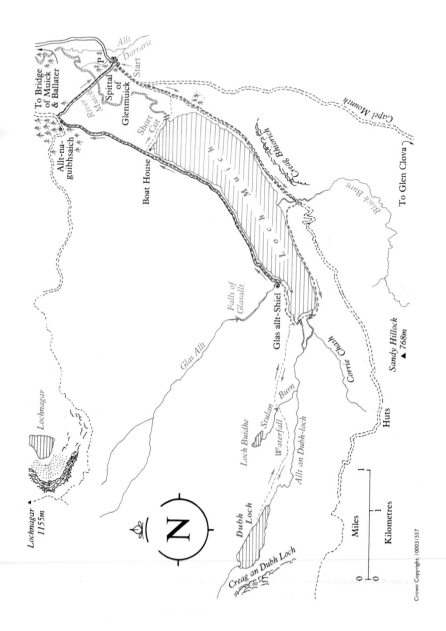

LOCH MUICK CIRCUIT

When Queen Victoria came to Balmoral in the mid 19th-century, there were no Royal lodges at Loch Muick, no motor cars, and no tourists. By the time of her death in 1901, however, there were signs that hill-walkers and climbers were beginning to make forays into the Deeside hills.

That process has accelerated over the past 50 years, and, as a positive response towards the management of both people and wildlife in the area, discussions between Balmoral Estates, local authorities and the then Countryside Commission for Scotland led to the establishment of the Glen Muick and Lochnagar Wildlife Reserve in 1972. So today, as another century begins, thousands of tourists head for Glen Muick in the summer months. For them, Loch Muick is one of the main attractions – the jewel in the Balmoral crown. This lovely stretch of water, 3km long, has become a firm favourite with walkers, and those with staying power can extend the Loch Muick Circuit by tramping another 3 km to the Dubh Loch.

From the Spittal of Glenmuick car park, cross the bridge over the Allt Darrarie and go down to the Visitor Centre, which will tell you all you want to know about the area. The centre is run by the estate with assistance from Scottish Natural Heritage and is staffed by countryside rangers. Winter is the best time to see the deer, when they feed at lower levels and can be seen from the tracks and paths. It is also worth coming in the late autumn, the rutting season, to hear the thrilling sound of the stags baying as they challenge each other for the right to mate with their chosen hinds.

A large key hangs on display in the window of the Visitor Centre. This was the key to the old hospice, or Spittal, that sheltered drovers and other travellers going over the Capel Mounth on their way south. The hospice stood where the track to the loch meets the track to Lochnagar. Take the route to the loch, keeping right where the Capel heads left, and walk towards a small woodland on the left.

INFORMATION

Distance: 11km (7 miles) circular. Add a further 8km (5 miles) for Dubh Loch.

Start and Finish: Spittal of Glenmuick. Take B976 from Ballater to Bridge of Muick and turn left on the Glen Muick road for 11km. This is a narrow road, with passing places, and is unsuitable for caravans or coaches. Please drive with care.

Terrain: Good tracks most of the way; narrower path on the east side of the loch. Boots recommended. Take waterproof and warm clothing.

Refreshments: None on route. Take food and drink with you.

Toilets: At the Spittal of Glenmuick Visitor Centre (see below).

Opening hours: Spittal of Glenmuick Visitor Centre, run by Balmoral Estates. Open all year round, daily during daylight hours. Ranger often present in the mornings.

Walkers heading for Loch Muick

The Capel was a major route to Glen Clova and the south. Jacobites, drovers, thravers – this ancient mountain pass has seen them all. It was probably the first hill track to see large numbers of bicycles, although mountain bikes had not been heard of when it happened. That was on a May day in 1892, when 16 cyclists went pedalling up the hill, the first to cross from Glenmuick to Glen Clova.

While the Capel climbs out of sight, your track runs on above the loch, under the rising slopes of Creag Bhiorach, with the surrounding hills mirrored in its placid waters. Loch Muick, which falls to a depth of over 90m, had good trout fishing at one time, although the trout were small. Two boats were used on the loch by Royal anglers in the 1930s, one for carrying people up the loch, the other for fishing. Old photographs show King George V and the Duke of York (later King George VI) making a sweep with a net.

Loch Muick attracts relatively little birdlife, but with luck you may see goosanders flying to and from the loch along the line of the river. A pair of red-throated divers has been seen on the loch in recent summers, but there have been no reports of breeding. Three kilometres from the Spittal is the Black Burn, whose peaty waters come frothing down into a lovely little bay. The burn is crossed by a wooden bridge. On the other side

Winter on Loch Muick

a rough track rises steeply up to the plateau, but your route is to the right, where a signpost points to the Loch Muick Circuit. A narrow footpath, stony and awkward in places, clings to the hill slope as it follows the loch to its sandy south-west beach.

Where the path turns across the head of the loch you pass another path which climbs steeply up by Corrie Chash to Alan's Hut (sometimes known as the Sandy Hillock Hut). Some people call this path the Streak of Lightning, and seen from the loch it certainly looks like that.

A stream called the Allt an Dubh-loch, which feeds Loch Muick, is bridged at various points as you cross the head of the loch to the Glas allt-Shiel track. Here, a path goes left to the Dubh Loch. For those who want to go to the Dubh Loch the following brief information may be useful:

The Dubh Loch (black loch) is 3km from Loch Muick, a little further if you go to the head of it. The path is very narrow in places and care has to be taken. At the loch itself the ground can be wet and boggy. The path climbs about 250m. On the right, halfway up, the Stulan Burn comes tumbling down from Loch Buidhe. Near the Stulan waterfall, a cairn marks the spot where the Marquess of Lorne proposed to Princess Louise on 3rd October 1870. Climbers are drawn to the Dubh Loch by the cliff face known as Creag an Dubh Loch. Some of Britain's top climbers have trained here before tackling Alpine or Himalayan peaks. Some walkers use the Dubh Loch as a route to get to the summit of Lochnagar.

If you are not taking in the Dubh Loch on your walk, follow the path from the head of the loch towards the woods at Glas allt-Shiel. This granite lodge – the 'shiel of the grey [or green] burn' – stands on a pine-covered delta and takes its name from a stream which drops down the steep slope behind it. It is a romantic spot, and at one time rhododendrons bloomed there. It was a favourite picnic spot of Queen Victoria and Prince Albert, and the Queen built the shiel after Albert's death. She called it her 'Widow's House'.

Reflections on Loch Muick

There is a by-pass path, which takes you through the woods to a narrow path leading up to Lochnagar by the Falls of Glas-allt, which are well worth seeing. The bypass takes you back on to a good track, which runs up the edge of the loch. In about 3 km you reach an old boathouse. From the boathouse a path provides a short cut across the end of the loch and over a footbridge crossing the River Muick to the Spittal track.

Ignoring the short-cut, carry on for about 2 km until Allt-na-giubhsaich (stream of the pines) is reached. This pine-sheltered lodge, fronted by yew trees and bright with rhododendrons early in the summer, looks out to Loch Muick. It was a sod-covered, one-chimney build-ing at the beginning of the 19th century, but by the time Victoria and Albert purchased Balmoral it had

Loch Muick from the Capel
Mounth, with Glas-allt-Shiel
on the right

become 'a most commodious cottage' known by its previous owner, Mr Gordon, as 'The Hut'. King George
VI spent a month here recovering from whooping cough
when he was a boy.

Beyond Allt-na-giubhsaich, turn right on the track back
to the Spittal. In the fields to the right – and occasion-
ally in the woods near the Visitor Centre – deer can
often be seen, but as the season moves on and visitors
begin to arrive, they shake off their winter ties with the
Spittal and head for the high tops.

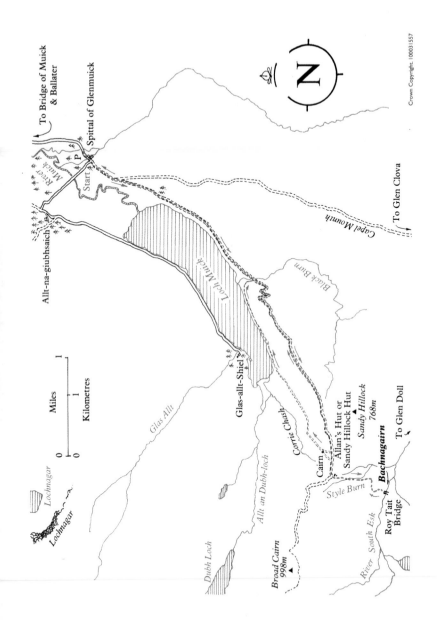

BACHNAGAIRN

The 'cleughs o' Bachnagaim' are at the end of this walk – a land 'where water rins and gowans blaw, and Grampian mountains busk their heids wi' snaw.' It is one of the more spectacular ways to cross the Grampians and it offers an alternative to the route by the Capel Mounth to Glen Clova.

As in the Loch Muick Circuit (Walk 12), the starting point is the Spittal of Glenmuick. For the first 3km you follow the track along the east shore of the loch to the Black Burn. Cross the bridge, and then go left up a broad, bulldozed track to the plateau. This is a hard push – so take it slowly. Once on top, the track runs south-west, keeping to the edge of the high ground above the loch.

Up there, beside a cairn at the top of the 'lightning streak' path, you have an eagle's-eye view of Glen Muick … the road coming down from Allt na-Guibhsaich, the dark cleft of the Dubh Loch path, the hills throwing their reflections into Loch Muick, and Glas-allt Shiel, where you may see tiny figures moving about the delta and wonder if the Royals are at Balmoral. From here, too, you will get a glimpse of a narrow path dropping steeply down Corrie Chash to the head of Loch Muick. This is the way you will return to the Spittal.

Bare moorland, riddled with peat hags, stretches out on your left as you continue along the track above what are known as the Loch Braes. The track bears gently away from the Braes and just under 3 km from the cairn on top of the zig-zag you come upon a corrugated-iron stable and shelter known as Alan's Hut or the Sandy Hillock Hut.

INFORMATION

Distance: 16km (10 miles) circular.

Start and Finish: Spittal of Glenmuick. Take B976 from Ballater to Bridge of Muick and turn left on the Glen Muick road for 11km. This is a narrow road, with passing places, and is unsuitable for caravans or coaches. Please drive with care.

Terrain: Good track to Sandy Hillock hut, then narrower path downhill to Bachnagairn. Steep return climb. Boots essential. Take waterproof and warm clothing with you, also OS Landranger map 44 and a compass. This walk should not be attempted by inexperienced walkers in poor weather conditions.

Refreshments: None on route. Take food and drink with you.

Toilets: At the Spittal of Glenmuick Visitor Centre (see below).

Opening hours: Spittal of Glenmuick Visitor Centre, run by Balmoral Estates. Open all year round, daily during daylight hours. Ranger often present in the mornings.

Climbing up from Loch Muick on the way to Bachnagairn

The Hut marks a mountain junction. About 200m before reaching it, you will see a resurfaced path on the right which goes down to Loch Muick by Corrie Chash. Note this for the return leg.

Beyond the Hut, the main track bears slightly right and goes on to Broad Cairn. If you want to 'bag' a Munro, Broad Cairn, whose summit is about 3km from the Hut, is a straightforward climb. But your route is down, not up, following a path that turns left just beyond the Hut and goes south beside the Style Burn to Bachnagairn. Other small paths run into the heather and fade away, so make sure you are on the Bachnagairn path – follow the line of the fence behind the Hut.

This narrow path drops towards the trough of the South Esk. Now you are really in the land 'where water rins and gowans (mountain daisies) blaw'. It is an idyllic spot. Dorothy Maria Ogilvy of Clova, an Angus poet, dipped into a rich broth of local dialect and painted a vivid picture of the the 'yammering yearn' (eagle) rising above the 'cleughs' (ravines) of Bachnagairn, seeking his 'wild wonnying' (dwelling place) on 'bauld Braidcairn'.

The downward path is fairly steep in places and in wet weather it can be slippery, so care is needed. Bachnagairn unveils its beauty slowly. First you see the fringe of the Bachnagairn firs, the slope of the hills east of the Tolmount pass, and, away to the left, the dark knuckle of Glen Doll. In this tree-lined setting of lofty crags and cascading waterfalls, the infant River Esk acts as an unofficial boundary between Deeside and Angus.

People come up from Glen Clova to picnic on this spot, crossing the bridge that spans the Esk. There is a sad, yet inspiring story about the bridge. When an Aberdeen man, Roy Tait, was killed on Lochnagar, his friends in Dundee, where he worked, decided to build a memorial to him – a bridge to replace a structure that was in poor repair. For months they worked on the project, taking beams and other heavy material partway up the hill by tractor, then carrying it the rest of the way on their backs. Now you cross the Roy Tait bridge when you step from Deeside to Angus. On the Clova side, you will see a plaque which says that the bridge was built by Roy Tait's family and friends and that he died on Lochnagar in August 1981.

A long strip of woodland drapes the banks of the river as it rushes down from Loch Esk, which is about a mile from the bridge. At Bachnagairn it drops about 20m in one great leap, through a ravine obscured by overhanging trees. Track and river chase each other down to the broad Clova valley, passing the point where the Capel Mounth comes in.

The bridge at Bachnagairn

Some people make the circuit from Loch Muick by Bachnagairn and back by the Capel to the Spittal of Glenmuick. That is a long, hard trail and not for us, but it is still worth crossing to the Angus side to explore Bachnagairn. Like Dorothy Maria, you may see 'whaaps (curlews), white hares, hoody craws and ptarmigan'. And wild flowers. The South Esk at Bachnagairn is a botanist's paradise.

Bachnagairn wasn't always deserted. There was once a shooting lodge there owned by Sir Allan Russell Mackenzie, 2nd Baronet in Glenmuick, and two fragments of a wall and the corner of a fireplace are buried in the grass about 100m from the bridge. The ruins of the stables are on the other side of the path.

So, no doubt reluctantly, you leave Bachnagairn and its magnificent setting and climb back to where Dorothy Maria could 'feel the wuns blaw frae the Capel Mount'. About 200m beyond Alan's Hut or the Sandy Hillock Hut, look on the left for the resurfaced path mentioned earlier, which goes down to the head of Loch Muick.

Here you have to make a choice. The Corrie Chash route opens up a superb view of Loch Muick, but it is sandy, very steep, tricky in places, and can be hazardous in wet or icy weather. The name means 'corrie of the difficulty', and that description could apply to the path as well as to the corrie itself, so considerable care has to be taken. You have to decide if you want to go back this way or to stick by the easier zig-zag route down the track to the Black Burn.

Either way, the last lap of the walk is along the east shore of Loch Muick, back to the Spittal.

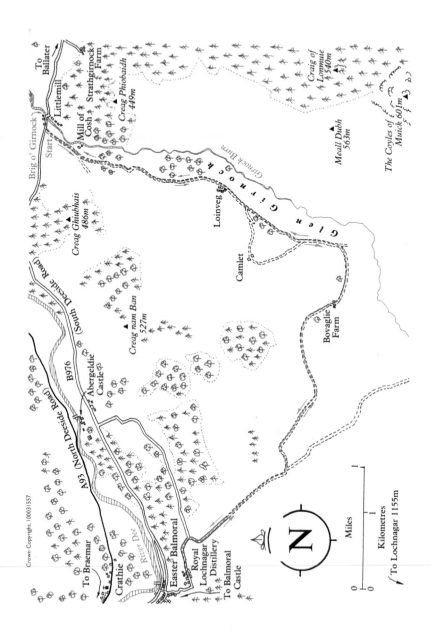

GLEN GIRNOCK

Whisky-smugglers and witches will be on your heels on this walk The starting point is Littlemill, 5 km west of Ballater, where the B976 does a sharp double twist over the Brig o' Girnock on its way to Balmoral. This lovely little hamlet, disturbed only by traffic avoiding the North Deeside Road, is at the mouth of Glen Girnock, or Strathgirnock as it is sometimes called. There is a farm of Strathgirnock about 1km east of Littlemill. The glen lies between two wooded hills called Creag Phiobaidh (piper's crag) and Creag Ghiubhais (pine crag), and the way into it from your parking place is by a track that follows the line of the Girnock Burn, passing an old mill on the left and a scattering of houses on the right.

It is a peaceful glen, yet it has had a curiously violent past. One of the most tragic feuds of the 16th century had its roots in Strathgirnock. The Forbes' of Strathgirnock and the Gordons of Knock had an undying hatred of each other. It reached a terrible climax when Alexander Forbes slew Francis Gordon, who wanted to marry Forbes' daughter. He later slaughtered Francis' seven brothers while they were cutting peat, then stuck their heads on their flauchters (peat-cutting spades). Forbes paid for the killings with his own life; he was tracked down and hanged on a tree in Strathgirnock.

When you clear the woods at Littlemill, the track runs past the foot of a hill called Creag nam Ban (the hill of the women), on the right. Here is another reminder of Strathgirnock's gory past. Witches were burned on the summit of the hill, the most famous of them being Kitty Rankine, 'French Kate', a maid at Abergeldie Castle. Whether or not the stories about her Black Magic are true is anybody's guess, but George VI stayed at Abergeldie Castle and both he and his brother David (later, briefly, Edward VIII) were led to believe as children that its bat-infested tower was haunted by Kitty Rankine's ghost. There is a post on top of Creag nam Ban which is supposed to be the stake where she was burned – and they say her screams can still be heard on dark winter nights.

INFORMATION

Distance: 12km (7miles) to Crathie. The walk can be shortened by turning back at Bovaglie Farm, which mkes it a 9km (5.5 miles) round trip.

Start: Littlemill. Take B976 west from Ballater. Littlemill is reached in about 5km. Park in the trees near the bridge. If walking to Crathie, you will have to arrange to be collected.

Terrain: Good tracks all the way. Boots or strong shoes recommended.

Refreshments: None on route. Tearoom at Royal Lochnagar Distillery (if open). Take food and drink with you.

Toilets: At the distillery.

Opening hours: *Royal Lochnagar Distillery:* May - Sept Mon - Sat 10.00 - 17.00, Sun 12.00- 16.00. Oct-April Mon- Fri 11.00-16.00. Visitor Centre, tearoom, guided tours and whisky tasting.

Bovaglie

It is a pity that Creag nam Ban has such a murky repu-
tation, for it is a lovely hill, wooded in places. Halfway
along its summit there is a group of trees known as
Jane's Firs, named after a woman who threw fir seeds
away there after the estate refused to give her the price
she wanted for them. There are also cairns scattered
about the top of the hill, including one in memory of
Queen Victoria's mother, the Duchess of Kent. The
cairn was erected after her death in 1861.

For those who want to climb the hill, the best approach is
from a back road branching off the B976 near Abergeldie
Castle. It can also be climbed from a number of points on
the track from Littlemill – the route of this walk – the
easiest and best place being at the deserted farm of Camlet.
Incidentally, look out for an old lime kiln at the roadside
near Camlet; it is in superb condition.

As you walk you will find that Strathgirnock, like so
many other Deeside glens, carries the scars of depopulation, and Camlet is one of a number of abandoned
farms. The first is Loinveg, about 2.5 km from Littlemill,
and Camlet is a kilometre further on. Its name comes
from An Cam-leathad, meaning 'the curved slope',
which is not a bad description.

The farm sits well off the main route, at the top of a track
that climbs up the hill from the glen road, then curves
back to it in a great loop. The folk who lived at Camlet,
cradled in the lap of Creag nam Ban, must have looked
across the moors that stretched endlessly in front of them
and felt that they were 'out of the world'. The rocky hill
immediately above the farm is Sgor na h-Iolaire, (the peak
of the eagle), but you are unlikely to see eagles there now.

Ahead, as you push up the glen, Lochnagar comes into
sight, and away to the left you can see the distinctive
grass-covered slopes of the Coyles of Muick. The word
Coyle comes from choille, meaning a wood, and these
'Coyles' are on the edge of a forest spreading up from
Glen Muick. There is, in fact, only one Coyle, the highest of three hilltops which stand out against the skyline,
but the name has come to be used collectively for the
group. The other hills are Meall Dubh and the Craig of
Loinmuie. The Coyles are part of a great belt of serpen-
tine rock which runs south-westward from the Moray
Firth through Deeside into Perthshire.

Just over a kilometre from Camlet, a smaller track branches left to the Girnock Burn, while the main track swings right towards the woods of Bovaglie. The shuttered windows of Bovaglie Farm tell the same old story. What was once a busy 'ferm toun' is dead and deserted. The great Strathspey musician, J. Scott Skinner, wrote a tune called Bovaglie's Plaid, inspired, it seemed, by a local saying that the wood 'haps (shelters) Bovaglie ferm like a plaid'. No longer. The 'plaid' is ragged now, bruised by the winds that whip across the featureless moors around it. This is the turning point if you wish to walk back to Littlemill.

From Bovaglie farm the track slopes up to join another track, where you go right to Easter Balmoral and the Royal Lochnagar Distillery, and on down to the South Deeside Road,

Glen Girnock was notorious for its illegal whisky-making. There were no fewer than a dozen 'black bothies' (illicit stills) in the upper part of this small glen. It is said that the remains of old stills can still be found in the glen. At one time you could see one at the back of Lochnagar Distillery, but it was a mock 'black bothy' constructed to show how whisky smugglers made their uisquebaugh (see picture right).

Whisky bothy at
Lochnagar Distillery

It was a whisky smuggler called James Robertson who turned 'legitimate' and opened the first Lochnagar Distillery in 1826. Queen Victoria liked the Lochnagar whisky, and frequently served it to her guests. It was delivered to the castle 'in bottles, with an attractive blue and black label, or more generally by the gallon in casks'. If you want to see a real distillery – and a legitimate one – you will find it at Easter Balmoral.

From the distillery, go downhill to the A976, turn right and after 50m left to cross a white suspension bridge over the Dee. Over the bridge, go straight ahead and shortly swing left towards the old manse of Crathie and the graveyard of the ruined church. It holds the gravestones of John Brown and several other royal servants, all erected by Queen Victoria to honour their service to her. Ahead, the road leads to the Tourist Information Centre, car park, and the main North Deeside Road at Crathie.

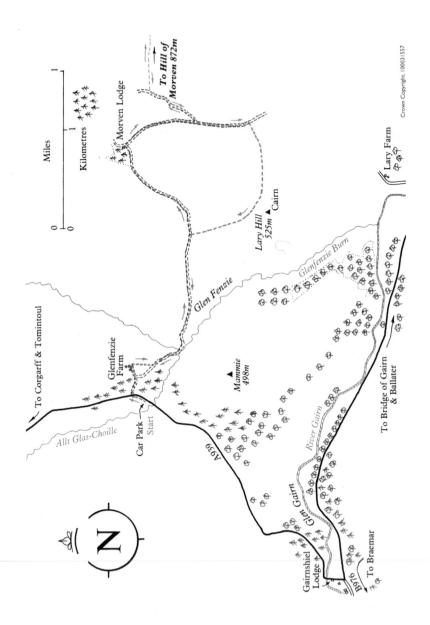

Crown Copyright. I0003I557

MORVEN LODGE

A spider's web of tracks converge on Morven – Mor Bheinn, the 'big hill' behind Ballater. One comes up the Deskry Water from Boutie's, the old drovers' inn at Boultenstone, near Tarland, while others push towards it from Logie-Coldstone, Tullich, the Pass of Ballater and Glen Gairn. The most attractive approach to the hill, however, is by a burn that comes tumbling out of the hills near Gairnshiel.

From the lay-by, walk up the road for about 150m and take a track on the right which goes uphill through a scattering of pine trees – this is the start of the route to Morven. Where it forks, go left around a loop that passes Glenfenzie Farm and rejoins the main track further on,

Glenfenzie is a ruin now, its roof shattered, its windows gaping to the sky, its outbuildings empty and deserted. Inside the house is a large 'swey' fireplace, conjuring up images of broth pots bubbling over a smoky peat fire. A swey was a movable, swinging iron bar from which pots and kettles were hung.

Outside, there are other reminders of the days when people lived here. On one of the granite stones on the front wall of the house are the initials 'DM' and the date 1879, while at the opposite end of the wall, another stone has the date 1822.

Whoever lived in Glenfenzie Farm in the 19th century had a magnificent view from the front window. The farm is perched on the side of a hill. From it you look down the long sweep of the valley, over a great rash of

INFORMATION

Distance: 6km (4 miles) circular, or 7.5km (5 miles) if Lary Hill is included.

Start and Finish: Layby on the A939. From the A93 between Ballater and Braemar, turn onto the A939 Tomintoul road. Cross Gairnshiel Bridge and continue for about 3km until you reach a green bridge beside a lone pine tree. Park beneath the tree.

Terrain: Mostly good tracks, but rough and indistinct path in places on Lary Hill. Boots rcommended. Take waterproof and warm clothing and OS Landranger sheet 37 and a compass.

Refreshments: None on route. Take food and drink with you.

Toilets: None on route.

Glenfenzie Farm

juniper bushes and across distant fields to the dome-like outline of Mount Keen.

As you follow the track downhill, the ruins of other build-ings can be seen. The Glenfenzie Bum cuts across the track and turns off through Glen Fenzie on its way to join the River Gairn. The burn has to be crossed by stepping stones, and from there the track goes left, climbing uphill towards a quarry. Lary Hill is on the right, another rough track rising towards the top of it from a point near the quarry. The track you are on continues uphill and then drops down towards the site of Morven Lodge.

The lodge stood in a green basin at the foot of the 'big hill', sheltered by pine trees. The track from Glenfenzie goes through this tiny wood, and deer can sometimes be seen grazing there. The lodge, owned by Alexander Keiller, the Dundee 'jam king' at the end of the 19th century, was an imposing building, bustling with life when the gentry gathered there during the shooting season.

In 1891, Keiller built a second Morven Lodge nearer Ballater and demolished the old one. Today, only traces of the original lodge can be seen, but there are still a number of abandoned buildings scattered about the grassy hollow where it stood – the stables, a laun-dry, the keeper's house and the shepherd's house. The pillared gateway at the entrance to the drive is a last link with Morven's lost glory. As for the 'new' Morven Lodge, it still draws hundreds of visitors, but they know it as the Craigendarroch Hotel and Country Club.

Morven itself is a great oblong lump of a hill. It is not part of this walk, but if you want to get to the 872m summit it is not too difficult. From the lodge you can see a track running along the side of the hill, and from there it is a comparatively easy climb up grassy slopes to the top. You should, however, be well equipped with waterproofs, boots, map and compass – the weather can change rapidly at any time of the year.

From the old lodge, the return can be made either by going back the way you came, retracing your steps to Glenfenzie Farm, or by going over Lary Hill, from where you will get marvellous panoramic views. If you plump for the Lary route, leave the lodge by the main drive, through the now

Laundry at Morven Lodge

redundant gateway, and take the estate road running south to Lary Farm. About 1.5km from the lodge you will come to a fence and gate. Beyond the gate, a rough path goes up Lary Hill on the right. This will take you over the hill and back down to the main track.

As you near the top of the hill the path disappears; just head for the highest cairn on the summit. From here you get a grandstand view of the Deeside hills: Morven behind you, Mount Keen in the distance to the south, Cairn Leuchan, the Coyles of Muick, Lochnagar and Ben Avon with its wart-like tors.

Place-name experts have different theories about the origin of the name Lary. Some say it may come from larach, a ruin, which seems improbable; the old Gaelic speakers in Glen Gairn said it came from lairig, a pass. This is more likely – Glen Fenzie, which runs along the foot of Lary Hill, was at one time a route taking travellers up by Laggan and on to Tornahaish and Strathdon.

Facing Lary Hill across the Glenfenzie Burn is another small hill with the curious name of Mammie which, although it has a maternal ring about it, simply means a little round hill.

From your bigger round hill, Lary, make your way down towards the Morven Lodge track. Keep to the right of the cairn and soon you will pick up the track that you first saw when you passed the quarry on the outward route. It is a rough, stony track, though quite wide, and care should be taken going downhill.

From the quarry, make your way back to the road and the parking place, missing out the loop to Glenfenzie Farm.

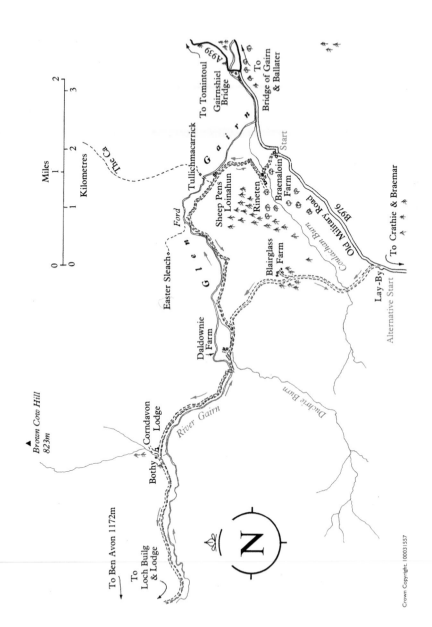

GLEN GAIRN

The glen of memories – that's Glen Gairn, whose river is the longest tributary of the Dee. From its source high on Ben Avon, the Water of Gairn flows east for over 30km until it reaches its outlet at a point called the Fit o' Gairn, near Ballater. Amy Stewart Fraser, whose book *The Hills of Home* became a best-seller and put Glen Gairn on the map, wrote about how this once well-populated glen had been emptied of its folk, leaving only larachs and deserted 'ferm-touns'.

The 7km stretch from the Fit o' Gairn to Gairnshiel is still well cultivated, but as you go west, life begins to ebb from the glen. It is near Gairnshiel, where a track stretches away to Ben Avon (pronounced Ben A'an), that this walk begins, not far from where the great hump-backed Gairnshiel Bridge loups the Gairn water and carries the old military road north to Corgarff.

There is no easy access to the track from the bridge itself, so it has to be approached from the roadside farm of Braenaloin, 1.5km south-west of Gairnshiel (10km from Ballater) on the B976 road to Crathie. Follow the Braenaloin track past the farm and go downhill to Rineten, where the path goes through a gate, turns right and then veers left towards the Gairn. You can join the track by a slightly shorter route branching off the Crathie road (see Information), but the Braenaloin route is recommended.

The track from Braenaloin is broad and clearly defined, running parallel with the river, and you follow it all the way to Corndavon and Loch Builg. Across the river is

INFORMATION

Distance: 14km (9 miles) circular. Add a further 10km (6 miles) for Loch Builg.

Start and Finish: Braenaloin Farm. From the A93 west of Ballater, turn right on A939. At Gairnshiel, in 6km, fork left. Braenaloin is 1.5km further on. Park carefully.

Alternative routes: There is another approach to Corndavon from the Gairnshiel-Crathie road. Halfway between Gairnshiel and Crathie, look for a large layby from where a wide, rough track goes down to a gate. This track crosses the Coulachan Burn and passes Blairglass Farm on its way to the Gairn, where it joins the track from Braenaloin near the ruins of Daldownie. This path can also make an alternative return to the road. Turn right after Daldownie Farm back to the A976.

Terrain: Generally good tracks. Boots or strong shoes recommended. Take waterproof and warm clothing with you.

Refreshments: None on route. Take food and drink with you.

Toilets: None on route.

Bridge over the Gairn

the abandoned farm of Tullichmacarrick, and not far away on the right is another ruin, all that is left of the minister's house. From this spot, a century ago, he walked to Sunday services in the kirk at the Bridge of Gairn, summer and winter, in wind, rain and snow.

There are sheep pens on the south side of the river, for Glengairn is sheep country. It is deserted now, but nearly a century and a half ago the manse, which was at an altitude of 370 m, looked down on a hamlet of six or eight cottages called Loinahun. One of the residents in Loinahun was an old weaver whose wife was a relative of John Brown, Queen Victoria's famous attendant. The Queen often gave gifts to cottagers on and around the estate, and more than once brought shawls, tea and tobacco to the old couple as she drove up the glen on her expeditions into the hills.

There is a bridge over the Gairn at Tullichmacarrick, and behind it a track climbs up the hill on its way to Corgarff. This is the Ca, the old route from Glengairn to Upper Donside. The name is an old Scots word meaning a way for cattle out to the rough ground, and rough it certainly is, for the path itself has almost disappeared in places.

As you make your way along the glen you pass the site of another farm, Easter Sleach, whose roofless farmhouse lay open to the winds for a long time. Now it has been demolished. It must have been a lonely place, high up on the hill, reached by a farm track from a ford across the Gairn. All along this stretch of the glen there are ruins marking the sites of former crofts and cottar houses, but you have to look for them. Ian Murray, in his book *In the Shadow of Lochnagar*, said he counted 75 recognisable dwellings in the glen.

The river, twisting and turning as it tumbles down from its head stream on Ben Avon, marks your route through the glen. About 3km from Braenaloin, the track begins to climb and the river loops away from it. Soon you will find yourself looking down on a grassy hollow where sheep graze near the ruins of Daldownie Farm.

Until it was demolished in 1977, Daldownie was the last farmhouse of any consequence in the glen. The folk there came to their door to wave to Queen Victoria as she rode past on her way into the hills, but all that is left of it now is a red-roofed barn and a rickle of stones – and maybe the fairies. The Daldownie farmer swore that there were fairies there. He heard their revels during the night and saw their footprints outside his house in the morning. There is a spot behind the house known as An Sidhean, the fairy hill.

Before the track drops down to Daldownie it meets up with another track coming in on the left – the alternative route from the Crathie road. Near the ruins it is carried over the Duchrie Burn by a small wooden bridge, while a little farther on there is a full-size iron bridge that, if things had been different, might have carried railway traffic from Ballater to Braemar. This bridge was built when an extension to the Deeside line was planned, and it should have crossed the river at the Fit o' Gairn. However, local landowners including Queen Victoria didn't like the idea and put a stop to it.

The Queen had reached an agreement with Captain Farquharson of Invercauld that the railway could be extended to Bridge of Gairn for goods traffic only, with a tramway from there to Invercauld. But the tramway was never built, so the railway bridge became a road bridge and was moved to its present site near Daldownie.

Upstream, not far from the bridge, are the remains of another failed project – what appears to have been a double dyke on the opposite side of the river. It is, in fact, a small channel that was to be part of a mill planned for this corner of Gairnside, but, like the Fit o' Gairn bridge, nothing came of it.

Restored Corndavon Lodge

Once over the Gairn bridge you are heading for lumpy Ben Avon. The track winds through scenery that becomes softer and gentler. But there is yet another ruin to see, although this one wasn't the result of depopulation. Corndavon Lodge, a shooting lodge for Royalty on the banks of the Gairn, was almost completely destroyed by fire. Only one corner of the original, extensive property now remains and this has been restored to make it habitable. The remaining parts of the ruin have been totally demolished. There is still the faint air of forgotten grandeur. Some trees remain on the rising ground behind the old lodge, which would have offered shelter from the north. Lord Cardigan, of Crimean War fame, was its tenant for a number of years, while in more recent times King George VI shot over the Corndavon moors.

Bothy at Corndavon, now closed because of vandalism

Close to the old Corndavon Lodge is a sizeable bothy. This is now securely locked against any use by walkers. This became necessary following acts of vandalism, so, sadly, this attractive stopping-off point is no longer available.

Corndavon must have been an impressive Royal 'howff' in its time, like so many other solid granite shooting lodges built in 'the back of beyond'. Some of the beds were hung with tartan which was said to have been at Culloden. In the large room which survived the fire, the walls have been decorated with a huge mural showing deer grazing in the hills around the Lodge. If you are tall enough you may be able to peep through the windows and see it.

Not far from the lodge is a hill marked on the OS map as Brown Cow Hill. In local dialect it is known as the Broon Coo. It is supposed to look like a brown cow, but it was once said that it looked more like a whale. When snow lies late in its corrie it is known as the 'Broon Coo's White Calf'.

The hills close in as you push up the glen and come to the last house on the walk – Lochbuilg Lodge. Not surprisingly, this is also a ruin. Donald McHardy, a stalker, lived here with his wife and family. The lodge stood on a knoll overlooking Lochan Feurach and Lochan Orr, two of a group of tiny lochans just before you reach Loch Builg. The loch marks the meeting place of a trio of vital routes through the hills; one through Gairnside (the route you have taken), a second by the Bealach Dearg, the Red Pass, to Invercauld and Braemar, and a third along a path by Loch Builg and Glen Avon to Inchrory and Tomintoul.

Loch Builg is a cold and desolate spot. There was a boathouse on the edge of the loch, by its south-western corner, used by hill-walkers and climbers going up Ben Avon, whose knotted brow looks down on this cross-roads in the hills. Reportedly someone had chalked across the wall, 'Welcome to the highest boathouse in the country. Peace and love to you all'. It was a nice friendly message to greet you at the end of a long trek. Now all that remains on the site are two small concrete slabs which formed the slipway to the loch; of the building nothing can be seen.

Here, on the shores of Loch Builg, we turn on our tracks and go back the way we came – back through the glen of memories. On the return there is the opportunity to take an alternative route by way of variation. Once past Daldownie Farm, take the right fork towards Blairglass Farm. Although this route is less attractive than following the Gairn, it does offer the possibility of excellent views into the corrie of Lochnagar. This is a view of Lochnagar which is seldom seen and those familiar with that mountain will be well rewarded. Once back on the road between Crathie and Gairnshiel, turn left to regain the starting point of the walk.

Loch Builg

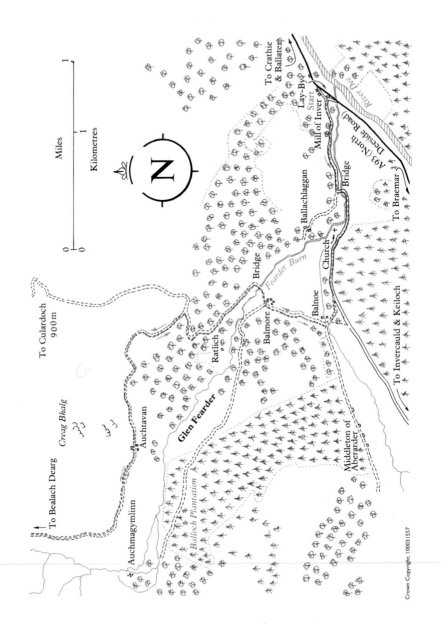

N

Miles

Kilometres

To Crathie & Ballater

Lay-By
Start

Mill of Inver

River Dee

A93 (North Deeside Road)

To Braemar

Ballachlaggan

Bridge

Church

Bridge

Fearder Burn

Balnoe

To Invercauld & Keiloch

Ratlich

Balmore

To Culardoch 900m

Middleton of Aberarder

Glen Fearder

Creag Bhalg

Auchtavan

To Bealach Dearg

Auchmagymlinn

Balloch Plantation

GLEN FEARDER

The grave of a giant – the last of his race – can be found in remote Glen Fearder on upper Deeside. At least that is what some people believe, and if you want to go giant-hunting, the place to start is at the Mill of Inver. Look for a signpost saying 'Aberarder'.

On the other side of the A93, at the mouth of the Fearder Burn, a narrow road goes up to Ballachlaggan, where 18 troublesome 'bonnet lairds' (tenant farmers) were once hung in the 'gryt barn at Aberardir' by order of the laird of Invercauld. Near a wooden bridge over the Fearder Burn a farm track leaves the road, crosses a cattle grid, and goes straight ahead to Ballachlaggan, but your route is over the bridge, following the line of the burn.

In about 1.5km from the main road you reach the old mission church of Aberarder, which became a school, then a storehouse for farm fodder. It is now a house.

The road meanders on through woodland to a junction where the main track goes left to Keiloch, at the entrance to Invercauld Estate, while you follow the right-hand branch down towards the farm at Balnoe. A newly built cairn awaits an interpretive board telling visitors more about the area; perhaps this will be in place by the time of your walk. The road splits again, one route turning left towards Middleton of Aberarder, where ruined cottages tell of more depopulation, and the other going on past Balnoe to the deserted farm of Balmore.

Your route is by Balmore, passing through a gate before reaching the abandoned farm. Beyond the farmhouse the road turns left and heads for the forestry plantation

INFORMATION

Distance: 9.5km (6 miles) circular. Add a further 1.5km (1 mile) for Auchnagymlinn.

Start and Finish: Mill of Inver layby on A93, 14km west of Ballater. About 3km after passing Crathie, look for a small cottage (an old tollhouse) on the right. The layby is just beyond it on the left.

Terrain: Good road to Balnoe, but once across the bridge at Balmore it is a rough track. Nearer to Auchtavan the track is rough and often wet. Boots recommended. Take waterproof and warm clothing with you.

Refreshments: None on route. Take food and drink with you.

Toilets: None on route. Nearest at Tourist Information Centre at Crathie (if open).

Auchtaven, nestling in the Deeside hills

at Balloch, but the route to Glen Fearder lies straight ahead, through a field with a red metal gate. The track runs down the edge of the field and leaves it by another gate. Make sure that you close all gates behind you (unless you found them open).

The track from Aberarder past Balnoe is an old droving route through the Gairn hills to the north. It went over the east shoulder of Culardoch to Loch Builg and from there on to Tomintoul. It became a public road at the end of the 19th century, but was eventually ousted by other routes.

Beyond the second gate at Balmore, the track crosses the Fearder Burn by a wooden bridge, meets up with a path from Ballachlaggan and swings left, climbing through thick woodland. The track here was bulldozed and widened in 2005. The going underfoot may be slippery until the track settles, so please take due care here. The new work stops at the dyke marking the boundary of Auchtavan land. There is another gate well up the hill. Look down through the trees on your left and you will see a ruined building not far from the Fearder Burn. This is all that remains of St Manire Chapel, near the farm of Ratlich. At one time a market was held there, but it moved to Clachanturn, near Crathie.

The track swings right and pushes uphill until it reaches a junction. The right branch is the old route to Culardoch, but your route is to the left, through a stretch of moorland where an amazing regeneration of birch trees has taken place. Here too, orchids and other wild flowers can be seen. The track gets rough, wet and muddy in places, so mind your step.

From this track you get a breathtaking 'back door' view of Lochnagar. It is different from any other view you may have seen of Deeside's famous mountain and when the clouds are chasing each other in and out of the gullies, it takes your breath away.

Near the dyke that marks the start of the Auchtavan lands, a number of ruined cottages point to the existence of a fair-sized community at one time. Another new cairn stands here, and this too should in time be accompanied by an information board. Note the kiln on the right-hand side of the track.

Nearby are the roofless shells of old 'black houses'. One building on the right did have a roof. It was made of corrugated iron, but when this was blown off a second roof was exposed – an old 'thacket' roof. The old roof has nearly all gone, but some remnants can still be seen.

The old chimneypot suffered from the Fearder gales. It was made of wood, as was the 'hingin' lum' inside the house. It sounds like a dangerous fire hazard, but the use of peat in the days of 'hingin' lums' made it reasonably safe.

The track comes to a high deer fence with a gate. From there it continues along the side of Creag Bhalg until it turns right at the head of Glen Fearder and wanders through the grey moors towards the old Bealach Dearg, the red pass, with another path cutting off to Culardoch.

Where the track turns north beyond Auchtavan, look down into the head of the glen and you will see a ruined settlement near the Fearder Burn. This is, or was, Auchnagymlinn, once the highest farm in the glen. Today the highest farm is Auchtavan, a name which in Gaelic means 'field of the two kids', an indication that the rent paid to the laird of Invercauld was two young goats.

Old cottage at Auchtavan, with thactched roof beneath a corrugated iron one

Fearder, on the other hand, means 'glen of the high water' or perhaps 'bog of high water', which says something about the conditions people there had to contend with in bygone days. It must have taken giants of men to carve a living out of this dour corner of the north-east. In fact, old tales suggest that they were giants.

The Deeside historian and writer A. I. McConnochie said you could see the grave of a giant at Auchnagymlinn – and that the grave was six metres long! There is another story, probably nearer to the truth. It says that members of a family which once lived in the forks of the Fearder Burn were all over seven feet (2.2m) tall, and that they all died young. It is unlikely that you will find any trace of giants now, for in the Muckle Spate of 1829, Auchnagymlinn was destroyed by sand and gravel.

Those with a liking for a long tramp can follow the Auchtavan track to the Bealach Dearg (crossing two burns on the way) and return through Invercauld to Keiloch and the A93, but car arrangements would have to be made. The easier way is to return the way you came, down to the old drove road and on by Balmore to Balnoe and Inver.

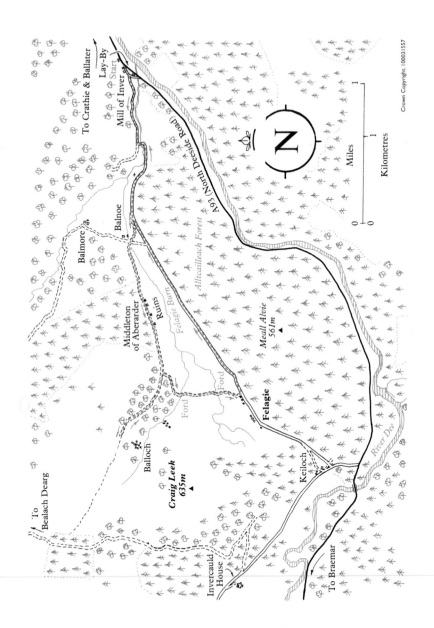

To Crathie & Ballater

Lay-By

Start

Mill of Inver

A93 (North Deside Road)

Balnoe

Balmore

Alltcailleach Forest

Middleton
of Aberarder

Ruins

Felagie Burn

Meall Alvie
561m

Ford

Ford

Ford

Felagie

Balloch

Keiloch

To
Bealach Dearg

Craig Leek
635m

River Dee

Invercauld
House

To Braemar

N

Miles

Kilometres

FELAGIE AND CRAIG LEEK

The Felagie Burn takes its name from the Gaelic *feith leaghaidh*, the slow burn. It wanders lazily through the district of Aberarder on the Invercauld Estate, near Braemar, which lies on the approaches to the Bealach Dearg, the red pass, once the main droving route to the south. It was a well-populated corner of Upper Deeside at one time.

The first part of the walk, past the old mission church of Aberarder towards Balnoe, is the same as in Walk 17. At the fork before Balnoe, turn left by a bridge crossing the Felagie Burn.

Here you follow an old track that runs by Middleton of Aberarder along the north side of the glen towards the 635m Craig Leek, a rocky hill east of the Bealach Dearg. The Aberarder track echoes with memories of the past, for at almost every step, crumbling ruins remind you of the time when people lived and worked in this quiet glen. The remains of their homes can be seen on both sides of the track, some in the fenced-off woodland on the right.

They are empty shells now, but in 1810 the school at Aberarder had no fewer than 120 pupils on the roll – 80 boys and 40 girls. By 1821 the number had dropped to 62, and when it closed a century later, there were only two pupils. In his book *The Old Deeside Road*, G.M. Fraser recalled that in 1921 you could 'find there scarcely a soul except at the few huts at Middleton'.

The first ruined house on the Middleton of Aberarder road was the old school before it moved to the mission church. Near this ruin an unlocked gate crosses the track.

INFORMATION

Distance: 8km (5 miles) circular. Add a further 3km (2 miles) for Upper Balloch settlement.

Start and Finish: Mill of Inver layby on A93, 14km west of Ballater. About 3km after passing Crathie, look for a small cottage (an old tollhouse) on the right. The layby is just beyond it on the left.

Terrain: Generally flat and easy going, apart from Craig Leek. Boots or strong shoes recommended. Take waterproof and warm clothing with you.

Refreshments: None on route. Take food and drink with you.

Toilets: None on route.

Deer feeding in Aberarder

Deer on track near Kelloch

Here, a large area of moorland has been fenced off to keep out the deer, enclosing the old clachan, and further up the track there is a gate on the deer fence with a metal catch. Make sure you secure the gate firmly behind you.

After this detour, follow the track towards Craig Leek until you come to a stream running down to join the Felagie Burn. A ford is marked on the map here. Local people used it when they crossed the moor to the south side of the glen, and this is your route back to Inver, but for the moment stick to the Middleton of Aberarder track as it bears right, uphill.

The track, which takes you to the ruins of two old settlements, is a continuation of a route, starting at Inver, which runs through the clachan of Middleton of Aberarder and climbs through a pass shown on old maps as Am Bealach (which simply means 'the pass'), eventually linking up with the Bealach Dearg. The Craig Leek track fades out as you climb, but when you come to a heap of stones on higher ground, bear left over a grassy area towards a line of trees on the ridge ahead.

The stones came from the 'steening' (stone clearing) of the land by the crofters, and piles of them can be seen scattered on various parts of the hill. This grassy hollow was at one time well cultivated, as the maps show, and the ruins of old holdings run hard into the gut of Am Bealach, sprawling uphill towards the road to the Bealach Dearg.

The two settlements were known as Upper and Lower Balloch, from *bealach*, a pass or hill-crossing, and in the higher settlement the clear line of a street can be picked out, with houses on either side. Some of the ruins lie on the opposite side of the burn which runs downhill through the settlements to the Felagie Burn.

From this high and windy spot you have an eagle's eye view of the Felagie glen. Craig Leek is said to be one of the finest viewpoints in the district, and it is easy to see why. From the track or from Craig Leek itself you look back on a breathtaking view of Lochnagar and the Stuic.

Up above the Balloch settlements a track curves away towards the Bealach Dearg. That way lies an alternative route to Keiloch and back to Inver, but it is not part of the present walk.

The return route is back the way you came, leaving the glories of Craig Leek and making your way down towards Aberarder and the Felagie Burn. Near the ford, keep an eye open for a tall flagpole marking the site of an old shooting range used in the time of the Boer War. Pieces of the targets can still be found scattered in the heather.

Ford the burn (a few easy steps) and make your way across the moor on a track crossing the Felagie Burn and linking up with the road from Inver. In winter the path over the moor can be wet and marshy – the burn is known as 'the bog-stream'. Once on the road, turn left for Inver. To the right lies Keiloch at the entrance to the Invercauld estate. There is an East Grampian Deer Management Group notice at Keiloch welcoming hill-walkers and visitors but asking them not to disturb the deer during the shooting season.

The road, which runs almost parallel to the A93, passes under the foot of Meall Alvie (560 m) and follows the line of Alltcailleach Forest. Some people say this was once part of the Old Deeside Road, and that it was also one of General Wade's military roads, but this has never been proved.

At any rate, it was a busy road, even being used as an alternative to the main Deeside road in the early days of motoring. Before that, in the latter part of the 19th century, it was repaired and linked up with the north route to the River Gairn by Balnoe and Balmore. The idea was to provide an alternative to the Bealach Dearg, avoiding the deer forests there.

There was also a Felagie village on this 'new' road, a group of about ten houses east of Keiloch. The village and its name can still be seen on some maps, and the ruins are there as a reminder of the lost' community. But all that is in the past. Middleton of Aberarder, the Craig Leek holdings and Felagie village have all gone. This long, wide glen and its lazy burn are left to the sheep and the deer. In winter, great herds of deer come down to the Felagie glen to be fed by the Invercauld keepers.

The walk along the south side of the glen is an easy one, taking you back to the old church at Aberarder and then down to your car at Inver.

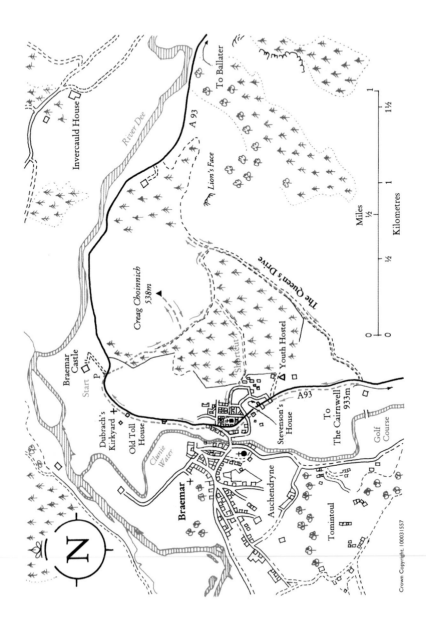

Invercauld House

River Dee

A 93

To Ballater

Lion's Face

Creag Choinnich
538m

The Queen's Drive

Braemar
Castle

Start

P

Dubrach's
Kirkyard

Old Toll
House

Clunie Water

Shortcut

Youth Hostel

Stevenson's
House

A93

To
The Cairnwell
933m

Golf
Course

Braemar

Auchendryne

Tomintoul

N

Miles

½   1   1½

Kilometres

0   ½   1   1½

THE QUEEN'S DRIVE

When Queen Victoria rode around Deeside in her carriage, she frequently followed an old track which ran along the side of Creag Choinnich. It was one of her favourite jaunts – and today the Queen's Drive is a popular walk, giving a grandstand view of Braemar and the surrounding countryside.

The starting point is a wooden gate opposite Braemar Castle. A finger post at the roadside says 'Braemar via The Cromlins' and is indicated as the yellow route. The Cromlins are fields between the village and Creag Choinnich.

Behind the gate a stepped path rises steeply away from the road, with fir trees on the left and birches bending their slender branches over the slopes of the Cromlins on the right. Down on the road an attractive cottage, once a toll-house, stands next to the ancient kirkyard where 'Dubrach' is buried.

'Dubrach' was Peter Grant, the last of the Jacobite rebels, who lived to be 110. His amazing story came to the notice of King George IV, who granted him a pension of £52 a year for life. 'Dubrach' remained an unrepentant rebel, declaring that if he had youth on his side he would 'fecht Culloden ower again'.

Take a breather at the viewpoint, which gives an excellent view of many of the Cairngorm peaks. The nearest is Morrone, behind the village, where you can pick out Tomintoul Farm (the name means 'hillock of the barn'), reputed to be the highest arable farm in Britain. There is also a board showing flora and fauna which can be

INFORMATION

Distance: 6km (4 miles) circular, including the ascent of Creag Choinnich.

Start and Finish: Car park close to Braemar Castle; the start point of the walk is across the road and a little further on. There are also car parks at St Andrew's Chapel and opposite the Invercauld Arms Hotel.

Terrain: Hill and woodland paths, some road at end of walk. Strong footwear recommended, particularly if climbing Creag Choinnich.

Refreshments: Wide choice in Braemar.

Toilets: In Braemar.

Opening Hours: Braemar Castle is open April to end October, 10.00-17.30, closed Fridays except in July and August.

Braemar from the viewpoint

Braemar from Creag
Choinnich

found on Deeside, including wildcats, squirrels, capercaillie, herons and eagles.

Continue along the path, following yellow waymarks. It levels out before reaching a gate where a stile takes you into the woods. The path narrows and the trees close in, but it is a lovely walk. At a T-junction, posts point downhill to the right, and uphill to the left – to Creag Choinnich. This is a stiff climb, not suitable for the unfit, but the reward is a spellbinding view of the Deeside hills. The path, shown by red waymarks, is broad until it breaks out of the woodland, where it narrows and climbs up the rocky dome to the summit at 538m (1764ft).

Here you can admire the view and ponder, perhaps, on the part this lumpy little hill has played in the area's history. Its name means 'Kenneth's Crag' and it was from here that Kenneth II (AD 971-995) once watched a hunt taking place. Here, too, the first hill race was held over nine centuries ago, when King Malcolm Canmore rewarded the winner with a purse of gold.

After the 1745 Jacobite Rising, the Redcoats occupied Braemar Castle, and before they left Deeside a cairn was erected on the north-west shoulder of Creag Choinnich, the inscription reading 'Erected by Edwin Ethelston Ensn, 25 Regiment, AD 1829'. Braemar Castle, built in 1628, burned down in 1689 and rebuilt about 1748, is owned by the Farquharsons of Invercauld.

From Creag Choinnich retrace your steps, past the two markers at the end of the Braemar Castle path. Look for the information on the Red Squirrel concealed in a fingerpost, then continue downhill until you see houses through the trees. If you want to shorten your walk, you can leave the track here, cross a stile, and return to the village, coming out near St Margaret's Church and making your way back to Braemar Castle.

For the full walk, follow the path as it bends left – at the bottom of the hill, close to the stile, there is a fingerpost indicating the way to the Lion's Face and Cromlins Circular Walk and again following the yellow route. Along this stretch of the path you will find another information post, this time with details of the Wood Ant. As you go through the woods the path forks, the way to the right following a more indistinct path.

Stick to the main path, going left, and climb gently until it comes to a T-junction where a sign points left to the Lion's Face. This is a crag high above the main road from Ballater to Braemar. The rocks on the upper part of it are supposed to look like a lion's head. The crag is now difficult to see because of the growth of trees on the steep slopes; also, time and weather have done their worst and you need a good deal of imagination to see the resemblance.

A track known as the Lion's Face Road runs round the south side of Creag Choinnich by Dubh Chlais (the black hollow), by-passing the village and coming out on the A93 Cairnwell road just south of Braemar. This was where Queen Victoria rode in her carriage, handing out money to children she met on the way – and so the track became known as the Queen's Drive. From the Lion's Face sign, walk a short distance along the Queen's Drive until you come to a seat overlooking Invercauld House and its policies. With its imposing central keep, the house, seat of the chiefs of Farquharson, almost looks like a castle. It was here that the Earl of Mar planned his Rising of 1715 and here, too, that 'Colonel Anne' Farquharson called out the clan for Prince Charlie. An information board gives more details.

Turn and head back the way you came. At the Lion's Face signpost note the ruins at the edge of the woods. An information post gives details of Mr and Mrs Thompson, the 'Friends of Queen Victoria', who stayed there, and were apparently visited by the Queen during her rides along the route. Continue along a wide track that will take you on to the Cairnwell road. It is a pleasant stroll and there are seats where you can sit and enjoy Deeside's magnificent scenery.

On reaching the road, go through the gate and turn right. On your left as you head into Braemar is the caravan site and Braemar golf course, which at 365m (1200ft) is the highest 18-hole course in Britain. As you enter the village, look for a house on the right with a plaque stating that here, in 1881, Robert Louis Stevenson wrote part of *Treasure Island*.

The last lap of the walk takes you by St Margaret's Church, past the Invercauld Arms Hotel, and on by the old toll-house and Dubrach's kirkyard to the Braemar Castle car park.

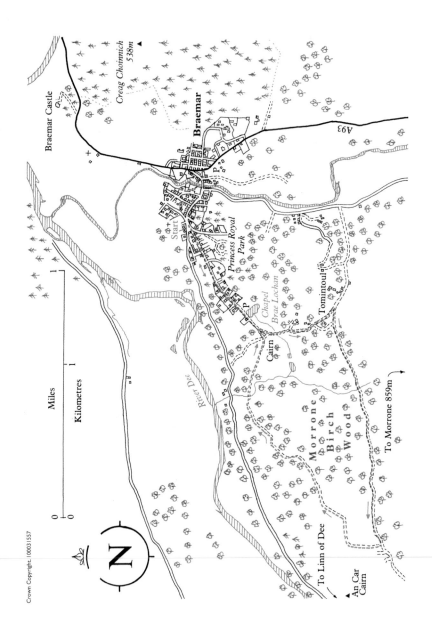

MORRONE BIRCH WOOD

One of the best examples of an upland birch wood in Britain can be seen on the lower slopes of Morrone, the 859m hill dominating Braemar. Its name, by the way, is another variation of Morven, meaning simply 'big hill'. There is a weather-recording station on the summit. The Morrone birch wood is designated as a National Nature Reserve by Scottish Natural Heritage.

This walk takes a pleasant clockwise circular route through the lower part of the wood and across moorland where there are good views down to the Dee Valley. Start from the west end of the village, near the Princess Royal park, where the famous Braemar Gathering is held each year on the first Saturday in September. Go to the foot of Chapel Brae, where an information board shows the various short walks around Braemar. Our walk is the 'Blue' route on the map. Go up Chapel Brae to the small lochan on the left, where there is a car park. The lochan, known locally as the duck pond, is the haunt of mallard ducks – wild birds, but tamed by tourism, for whenever a car appears they come waddling over looking for titbits.

On the track that passes the pond there is a sign saying 'Morrone Birch Wood'. Follow the track and go through the gate at a cattle grid. A fingerpost indicates the way to the Morrone Birch Wood. Turn left, up the hill, following the marker posts with blue bands, and past the house called Woodhill. Continue up the hill until the track forks to the right; go initially to the left to reach a superb viewpoint – a good place to survey the surrounding

INFORMATION

Distance: 5km (3 miles) circular.

Start and Finish: Princess Royal Park, Braemar.

Terrain: Woodland paths and tracks. Some sections can be muddy in wet weather. Boots or strong shoes recommended.

Refreshments: Wide choice in Braemar.

Toilets: In Braemar.

Opening Hours: Braemar Tourist Information Centre and Heritage Centre open all year, 0930-1730 daily in summer, but more limited hours from September to May.

Looking along Glen Quoich
from the viewpoint

countryside, including the big hills of the Cairngorms, before continuing the walk. The various hills can be picked out on an indicator erected by the Deeside Field Club in 1960 to commemorate their 40th anniversary. On the top are four lines of verse by a former Lord Provost of Aberdeen, the late George Stephen. The continuation of this track goes up to the summit of Morrone, perhaps to be tackled on another day.

This part of Morrone is known as Tomintoul. The Banffshire Tomintoul claims to be the highest village in the Highlands but, not to be outdone, the Braemar Tomintoul once claimed to have the highest arable land in the country. The Gaelic origin of Tomintoul is Tom an t'Sabhail, the hill of the barn. The name was given to the highest of a group of crofts on Morrone, and it came to be applied to the whole group.

A rushing burn in Morrone birch wood

Having admired the view from the indicator and possibly taken a rest on the welcome seat nearby, go back to the junction of the tracks and now go left, heading west along the upper track in the Birch Woods. This path is fairly flat and continues for about 1.5 km, offering good views across the great sprawl of moorland and over the birches. Look behind you to see the rooftops of Braemar. To the east is Creag Choinnich – Kenneth's Crag – the hill on the outskirts of Braemar, named after King Kenneth II. Its 538m summit is a splendid viewpoint (see Walk 19).

The path goes through the wood, giving more fine views of the hills across the Dee. In early summer, alpine plants carpet the ground and later the heather turns to purple, splashing Morrone with colour. But it is the 'dainty lady' of the forest, the silver birch, that holds sway. The birch is small, sometimes no more than 5m in height, and seldom more than 10m. The Morrone Birchwood extends up to over 600m on the northern slopes of the hill, and at its upper edge it is close to the maximum altitude for tree growth.

Juniper bushes proliferate beside and beneath the birch, creeping across the hill as if intent on taking it over. There is a dense growth beneath much of the wood and heavy thickets where the trees thin out. The path pushes on crossing various burns, gurgling down from springs on the hill. In spate, these little burns can be tricky to cross and the going on the path itself can be wet after rain.

You reach a gate and, going through, leave the area protected from the deer. Both red deer and roe deer can often be seen both inside and outside the exclosure. The exclosures were fenced off in 1978 to protect the trees from the browsing deer. The plan was to remove the fences at a later stage and to repeat the operation at other points to encourage regeneration. Note the slats attached to the fence, these were added more recently and improve the visibility of the fence especially for the rare capercaillie, which can be injured or even killed by flying into the fence.

Deer feeding in Morrone birch wood

Along the path look ahead and slightly right to see Glen Quoich. In the distance you will see a cairn sticking up above the trees beyond the fence. This is An Car, or the Car Prop as it is known locally (a prop is a prominent landmark), and it was at one time popular with visitors, but is now almost swallowed up by the trees.

The path continues until it reaches the edge of a wood where a stile would allow access. However, this is the limit of our walk and we do a U-turn to follow the path slightly downhill and back towards Braemar. On the return walk the path is lower and narrower and again crosses burns, some of which offer stepping stones in order to cross without getting wet. Eventually you reach the gate where you entered the reserve; go through and soon reach the duck pond and the return down Chapel Brae.

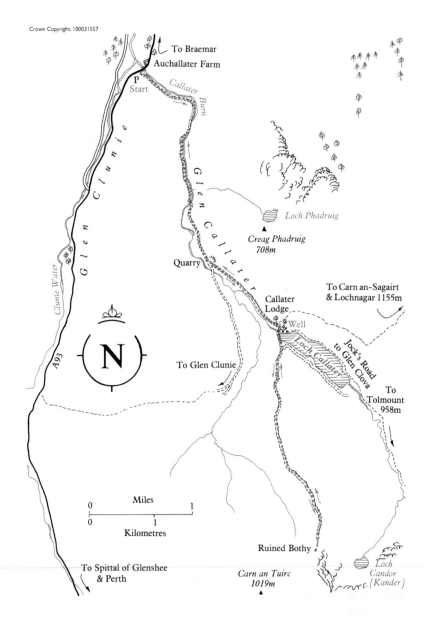

Crown Copyright. 100031557

To Braemar
Auchallater Farm
P Start
Callater Burn
Glen Clunie
Clunie Water
A93
Glen Callater
Loch Phadruig
Creag Phadruig
708m
Quarry
To Carn an-Sagairt
& Lochnagar 1155m
Callater
Lodge
Well
N
To Glen Clunie
Loch Callater
Jock's Road
to Glen Clova
To
Tolmount
958m

Miles
0   1
0   1
Kilometres

Ruined Bothy

To Spittal of Glenshee
& Perth

Carn an Tuirc
1019m

Loch
Candor
(Kander)

LOCH CALLATER

Loch Callater was once described in an official Deeside survey as an 'idyllic' place. It was not an overstatement, for this is one of the loveliest lochs in the area. From it, paths stretch away to Carn an t-Sagairt and Lochnagar, up by the windy wastes of the Tolmount to Jock's Road and Glen Clova, and onto a high plateau where Prince Albert put a message in a bottle and stuck it in the ground for future generations to discover.

From the car park at Auchallater, a Scottish Rights of Way Society sign points the way, and up a short, stony brae a gate with access for walkers opens up your route through Glen Callater, following the course of the Callater Burn. Here, Nature has sculpted the river rock into weirdly impressive shapes, jagged splinters of stone contrasting sharply with long, flat table-tops worn smooth by the endless motion of the burn.

The rocks are mostly of micra-slate and granite. Micra-slate was at one time quarried at the lower end of the glen for roofing. The whiter-than-white stones you see in ditches just off the track are limestone, which is more prevalent at the north-west end of Loch Callater.

The glen is hemmed in by high hills. Halfway up there is supposed to be a green hillock inhabited by the 'little folk'. Professor William MacGillivray, a noted 19th century Aberdeen naturalist who roamed these hills and glens, reported in 1850 that a man still living had seen fairies dancing on the hillock, with a piper playing to them.

Myth and magic breed easily in these lonely straths. Callater should really be Patrick or Peter's Glen, for a number of landmarks in and around the glen are called after a priest of that name. About halfway along the glen, where a wooden bridge crosses a burn coming down from the hills on the east, a barely visible path runs alongside it up towards Loch Phadruig.

INFORMATION

Distance: 10km (6 miles) circular. Add a further 6km (3.5 miles) for Loch Kander.

Start and Finish: Auchallater, on A93 3km south of Braemar.

Terrain: Good track all the way to Loch Callater. Rough, steep path up to Loch Kander. Boots recommended. Take waterproof and warm clothing and OS Landranger sheet 43.

Refreshments: None on route. Take food and drink with you. Wide selection in Braemar.

Toilets: None on route. Nearest in Braemar.

Dark Loch Candor (Kander)

This tiny loch, hiding behind Craig Phadruig, can't be seen from the glen, but both loch and crag are named after Peter the Priest. Carn an t-Sagairt, which is reached by a path from Loch Callater, is 'the priest's hill'. All this stems from a miracle performed by Peter when the Braemar area was in the grip of a severe frost that lasted into May.

When a holy well at Loch Callater froze over, leaving the people without water, they called in Peter the Priest. He prayed, the ice melted, and water trickled from the well. Then, as he prayed on, clouds gathered over Carn an t-Sagairt, the frost loosened its grip on the land, and a thaw set in.

Loch Callater

The track through this 'miracle' glen is uninterrupted until you come to a quarry on the left. Here the track forks, the right-hand branch going off to Glen Clunie, and the left, which you stay on, to Loch Callater. Soon you will see birch trees rising above an old gamekeeper's lodge near the lochside. The track runs past a gate leading to the front of the lodge, while another track goes behind the house.

Callater Lodge looks out over the loch, which runs south to where deer come down from the high tops to graze on grassy haughs below the Tolmount. The loch, which lies at an altitude of 500 m, is about 1.5 km long and covers an area of about 30 hectares. Gulls squawk and dive over its surface and if you are lucky you might see a skein of geese flying low over the water.

Sitting on the grass outside the lodge on a sunny day, looking away to the distant hills, the Deeside survey's description of the scene as ' idyllic' seems to sum it all up. However, the lodge is boarded up and stripped of its porch, a rather sad sight.

But life has come back to the nearby stables. In 1993 volunteers from the Mountain Bothies Association restored the building for use as a bothy. Now it provides simple shelter for walkers heading over Jock's Road to Glen Clova, or coming the other way. The path to Clova goes along the east side of the loch, passing a large stone which marks the site of Peter's Well, the scene of Callater's miracle.

From the lodge, looking across a wooden bridge that spans the Callater Burn, a steep, stony track can be seen zigzagging up the steep hill that flanks the loch on the west. This track goes up towards Carn an Tuirc ('hill of the boar') and on to a plateau from which you can look down on a remote mountain loch described by one writer as 'lovely, lonely dark Loch Kander'.

The track is easy to follow for most of the way, but it peters out on the plateau. The ground drops away steeply on the left and as you head towards the corrie above Loch Kander, look for what appears to be a pile of stones some way ahead. This is all that remains of an old shepherd's bothy that once looked down on Kander, a rough but-and-ben perched high over what William MacGillivray called 'a recess in the bosom of a mountain'.

It is a fairly steep climb and should only be attempted in good conditions by fit walkers, but for those who make the climb, the rewards are great. The views are breath-taking, but even more fascinating is the glimpse you get of Loch Kander, an inky pool far below you. William MacGillivray estimated that the depth of the corrie was about 245m.

He noted that there was a place in the bothy for a small fire, two stone benches, and two recesses in a wall for pipes and other articles. The bothy is now a roofless ruin, but one of the benches can still be seen – and there is still a hole in the wall for the shepherd's pipe.

It can be cold in these high places. When Queen Victoria was there, taking a look at Loch Kander and describing it as 'very wild and dark', she found ice thicker than a shilling coin. It was somewhere near Carn an Tuirc that Prince Albert wrote a message on a bit of paper, put it in a water-bottle, and stuck it in the ground.

You can also make a low-level approach to Loch Kander by walking along the west side of Loch Callater, but the track gives way to a narrow footpath at the end of the loch and finally disappears. Moreover, as you near the opening to Loch Kander the ground becomes wet and boggy.

Whether you make Loch Callater your turning-point, or climb the zigzag track to peer down at Loch Kander, it's a fair bet that you will want to return to this lovely area, for Callater is being 'discovered' by an increasing number of discerning walkers.

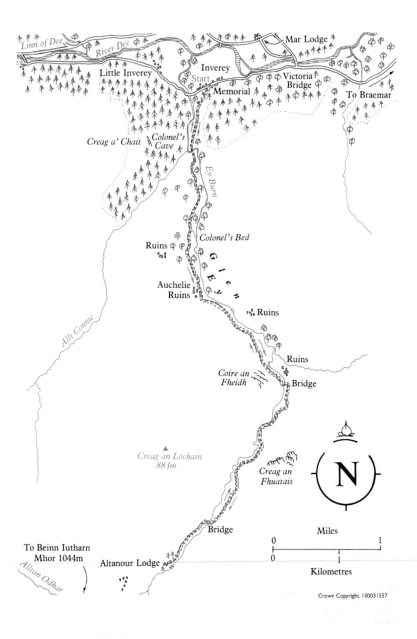

Linn of Dee
River Dee
Mar Lodge
Little Inverey
Inverey
Start
Victoria Bridge
Memorial
To Braemar

Creag a' Chait
Colonel's Cave

Ey Burn

Colonel's Bed
Ruins

Glen Ey

Auchelie Ruins
Ruins

Allt Connie

Ruins

Coire an Fheidh
Bridge

Creag an Lochain 883m

Creag an Fhuatais

Bridge

To Beinn Iutharn Mhor 1044m
Altanour Lodge

Allt an Odhar

N

Miles
0   1

Kilometres
0   1

Crown Copyright. 100031557

GLEN EY

The mountains of hell – that was what Deeside folk called the two peaks, Beinn Iutharn Mor (1044m) and Beinn Iutharn Bheag (951m) at the head of Glen Ey. In between them is the source of the Ey Burn, which runs down the glen for 12km until it reaches Inverey and the River Dee.

Inverey was where a legendary character called Maggie Gruer lived. In her home at Thistle Cottage, she gave shelter to hundreds of walkers and climbers in the 1930s. She was known to all manner of folk, poets, playwrights and politicians among them, and her homemade oat-cakes and thick scones were talked about wherever outdoor folk met. Maggie charged a shilling (5p) for bed and breakfast, or sixpence (2½p) if you were hard up, and she kept the money in a bucket.

The track into the glen starts almost opposite Maggie's house, near a memorial to John Lamont, a native of Inverey, who became the Astronomer Royal of Bavaria. It goes up past a modern house, through a gate, and after crossing a wooden bridge over the Ey Burn, climbs towards a hill on the right.

There was a wood on the hill at one time, but it has virtually disappeared, leaving only a handful of shattered trunks and stumps. Why it died is a mystery, but it may simply have been devastated by the fierce winters in the glen. The same sort of devastation can be seen at Altanour, 8km up the glen, which is the turning-point of the walk.

This bare, scabbed hill adds a sense of desolation to a glen that still carries the scars of the Clearances, when crofting families were evicted to make way for deer. Five families were moved out in 1829 and resettled elsewhere on the estate. Another eight families were evicted in 1842, along with 3,000 sheep and cattle. A clampdown on illicit whisky distilling speeded up the depopulation, for without this extra income the crofters were unable to pay their rents.

INFORMATION

Distance: 16km (10 miles) circular.

Start and Finish: Inverey, 6 km west of Braemar on the Linn of Dee Road. Use the new car park located in Inverey on the south side of the road.

Terrain: Good track all the way to Altanour Lodge. Boots or strong shoes recommended. Take waterproof and warm clothing with you.

Refreshments: None on route. Wide selection in Braemar.

Toilets: In Braemar or at Linn of Dee.

Altanour ruins

Professor William MacGillivray, in his *Natural History of Deeside and Braemar*, published in 1855, describes middle Glen Ey as 'a fair green strath, smooth as a well-kept lawn', but he added that there was not a single sheep to be seen. He thought the glen as beautiful as an English park, and in many ways it still is, but the crumbling ruins of deserted settlements give it an air of sadness.

The Colonel's Bed

About 2km from Inverey, a small wooden sign at the left edge of the track points to a path that will take you to the Colonel's Bed. It was here, in a narrow ravine on the Ey Burn, that John Farquharson of Inverey, a freebooter better known as the Black Colonel, hid from government troops in 1715.

The path is narrow and in wet weather can be muddy. Where it drops down to the mouth of the Colonel's hiding-place it is often slippery and dangerous. It is inadvisable to take children down here. The 'bed' is a long ledge of slaty rock, though recent rockfalls make identification of the actual 'bed' difficult. It is an awesome place, yet it has its own beauty. Its high, perpendicular cliffs are covered with ferns and flowering plants.

Beyond the Colonel's Bed, the glen becomes green and fertile, with dyked fields spreading out on either side of the track. Now you are in MacGillivray's 'fair green strath', perhaps the loveliest part of the glen, but here too are reminders of the years of eviction. Up on the right you will see the larachs, the crumbling ruins of old settlements.

Two large ruins can be seen above the track at Auchelie, looking down over the Ey Burn. Two tall larch trees stand outside the houses, untouched by the storms that have stripped so many other trees in the glen. Climb up the hill behind them and you will get a striking view of the Ey Burn as it curves away to the hills at Altanour. The name Auchelie comes from Ach a'Chleiridh, which means 'the field of duskiness'.

The main settlements lay on the opposite side of the river between Auchelie and Creag an Fhuathais, a high, pyramid-shaped hill where the river turns south-west to Altanour. Creag an Fhuathais means 'crag of the spectre', and there is an old tale that a malicious ghost rolled huge stones down on passers-by, and that something seemed to move along the hillside -'loathsome, black, shapeless, monstrous' is one account.

Near the foot of Creag an Fhuathais, a wooden bridge which spans the Ey Burn leads to the ruined settlements, which can be seen spreading out on the left. It was among these pathetic ruins that many families lived out their lives in peace until the evictions came. The townships contain the remains of a number of corn-drying kilns, and there are longhouses divided into two or three rooms. In one empty shell you can see flagstones on the ground.

To continue the walk go back to the bridge, where the main track now goes up the east side of the Ey Burn. The river, wriggling and curling through the moorland like a silver serpent, is on your right, and across the water is Corrie an Fheidh – the corrie of the deer. It is well named, for you can often see herds of deer grazing here.

The hills close in as you walk towards Altanour, the Ben Uarns, as they are sometimes called, forming a crescent at the head of the glen. Eventually another bridge takes you back to the west side of the river for the final stretch up to Altanour.

The old shooting lodge takes its name from Alltan Odhar (the dun burn), a tributary of the Ey Burn. The lodge is a sad sight now, so ruinous that there is little left. The wood which sheltered it has met the same fate, withering away as if stricken by some terrible disease. Dead trees lie all around, and many people find this an eerie spot.

Beyond Altanour are more ruins, all that is left of the summer sheilings used by the crofters. Deeper still into the glen are the 'mountains of hell', where you may see eagles quartering the sky. Your way, however, is back down the glen, past the corrie of the deer and under the brooding brow of Creag an Fhuathais, where people once fled from a ghost which 'made their hair stand on end and their flesh creep with inexpressible horror'.

Despite the ghost, the ruins and the dying trees, Glen Ey is a delightful place in which to walk. Your only regret will be that there is no Maggie Gruer waiting at Inverey to pour you a cup of tea from her ever-ready teapot and to offer you thick scones and home-made oatcakes.

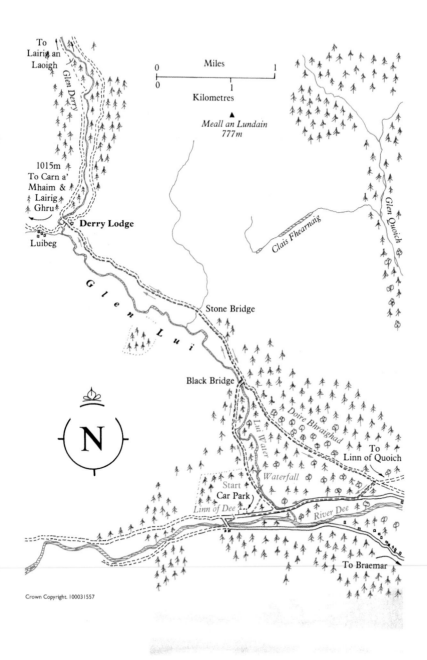

To
Lairig an
Laoigh

Glen Derry

0   Miles   1

0   Kilometres   1

▲
Meall an Lundain
777m

1015m
To Carn a'
Mhaim &
Lairig
Ghru

Derry Lodge

Luibeg

Clais Fhearnaig

Glen Quoich

G l e n   L u i

Stone Bridge

Black Bridge

Doire Bhraighad

Lui Water

To
Linn of Quoich

N

Waterfall

Start
Car Park

Linn of Dee

River Dee

To Braemar

DERRY LODGE

When Queen Victoria opened the bridge over the Linn of Dee on 8th September 1857, she drank a glass of whisky to its future 'prosperity'. She could never have imagined what that prosperity would mean 150 years later – sightseers crowding the banks of the Linn to see the spectacular waterfalls, cars jamming the approaches to the bridge, and backpacking walkers tramping off into the hills.

The Linn is the southern gateway to two great Cairngorm passes, the Lairig Ghru and the Lairig an Laoigh. This walk takes you to the doorstep of them both and gives a taste of the mountain massif that sprawls so magnificently between Deeside and Strathspey.

Before setting out, however, it is worth taking a look at the Linn. Here, the River Dee rushes through a narrow channel, only a metre or so wide, cut in the schistose rocks and opening out into a series of great circular pools. Leave your car at the large car park built inside the trees a short distance from the bridge. This is the starting point for the walk.

In the car park are signs saying 'To Glen Lui'. They mark the start of a shortcut to the glen and the Lodge. Where the shortcut ends, turn left on the track. Now you are in Glen Lui, on the road to Derry, following the Lui Water to the Black Bridge. The first part of the walk is probably the loveliest, with the Lui surging and cascading through a series of beautiful pools, over great rock steps and down turbulent falls. It is in sharp contrast to the bare mountain scenery at the other end of the glen.

INFORMATION

Distance: 13km (8 miles) circular.

Start and Finish: Linn of Dee, 10km (6 miles) west of Braemar. There is a large car park near the bridge (current charge £2).

Terrain: Good tracks or paths all the way, but boots are recommended. Take waterproof and warm clothing with you.

Refreshments: None on route. Take food and drink with you.

Toilets: At the car park at Linn of Dee.

Black Bridge and Derry Cairngorm

The 77,000 acre Mar Lodge Estate was acquired by the National Trust for Scotland in June 1995, and is now held by the Trust on behalf of the nation, and managed with conservation as the primary aim.

Some people wonder what dark story lies behind the name Black Bridge, but it is called that simply because it was once tarred. Here, as the glen opens up, you go left at the bridge, along a track that was until fairly recently fringed on one side with ancient pines which spread up the hill slopes on your right. Now they are gone, but new trees are regenerating well in their place. Watch out for a burn coming down from the right and running under an old stone bridge to join the Lui. You will see a narrow path climbing up the hill This leads through Clais Fhearnaig to Glen Quoich (see Walk 24).

Glen Lui was one of the main routes linking the high passes of the Lairig Ghru and Lairig an Laoigh with Deeside, and as you go up the glen, you pass the ruins of old dwelling-houses at the roadside. The only permanent residents now are the deer. In Glen Lui, if you are lucky, you will see great herds of red deer grazing on the grassy haughs beside the Lui Water. Up on Meall on Lundain, on your right, a line of stags can sometimes be seen on a high ridge above the track, watching the passing walkers. They will wait until the coast is clear and then come down to join the herd by the river.

Luibeg and the track to the Lairig Ghru

As you near Derry Lodge, go down a track on the left. On reaching the river you can see Luibeg, where deer are often seen grazing. This remote cottage, now shut up, was once the home of a legendary keeper, Bob Scott, who gave shelter to hundreds of walkers coming out of the Lairig Ghru. They slept in a bothy outside his house, but it was burned down some years ago. A replacement was built a little way down the Lui, but this too was burned down in 2003. Now a new bothy has been put up, opened for use in summer 2005.

It has been said that Lairig Ghru means 'the gloomy pass' and certainly this steep-sided pass, rising to a height of over 800m, can be dark enough. However, the name may come from the Allt Dhru or Druie, the burn on the northern side of the pass which leads down through the great forest of Rothiemurchus and eventually to Aviemore. The Lairig an Laoigh is the 'pass of cattle', indicating that this was once an important droving route.

Go back to the main track and turn left to Derry Lodge. Not so long ago the approach was through a large area of pines, but most of the trees have gone. Derry Lodge itself is boarded up, and the interior is falling into ruin. The lodge was at one time a focal point for hill people. It was leased to the Cairngorm Club for a time in the 1950s, but high rents forced them to give it up.

In the open ground beyond the lodge is a wooden building used by the Aberdeen Mountain Rescue Team, with an emergency telephone on its wall. Nearby, a wooden bridge that spans the Derry Burn has a concrete block with the names of the 19 volunteers from Aberdeen University OTC who built it. The names are becoming difficult to read. A signpost points the way to the two Lairigs and back to Braemar.

This is a good place to eat your sandwiches and contemplate the Cairngorms. You are on the doorstep of this great mountain range. From here and across the bridge, a track winds its way round Carn a'Mhaim on its way into the Lairig Ghru. To the north lies Glen Derry and the Lairig an Laoigh.

Leaving the lodge, go back through Glen Lui to the Black Bridge, but instead of crossing it, continue on the track that climbs uphill through the Doire Bhraghad, a fir wood whose name means 'copse of the upland place'. From this hill there is an impressive view looking south up Glen Clunie, while ahead you can see across the Dee to Inverey and the hills beyond it. The lodge at the entrance to Glen Ey and the track pushing south through the glen to Altanour (Walk 22) can be picked out as you walk along this 'upland place'.

There is a steep climb after passing the Black Bridge, but it then becomes an easy, pleasant walk. Below, through the trees on the right, is the road from the Linn of Dee to the Linn of Quoich. About 2km from the Black Bridge a track cuts back and goes downhill, onto the Quoich road. Go right, and a walk of about 1.5km will take you back to the car park at Linn of Dee.

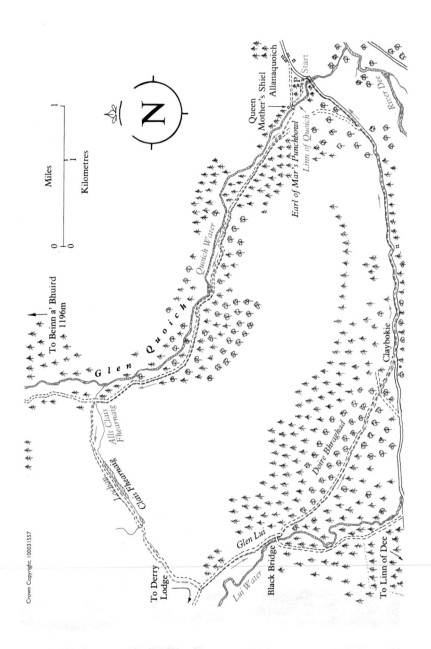

GLEN QUOICH

Although the Linn of Dee is one of Deeside's most popular attractions, another waterfall only 6km away has its own special appeal. This is the Linn of Quoich, on a tributary of the River Dee, and from there this walk goes to a hidden glen on the edge of the Cairngorms.

The Earl of Mar's Punch Bowl is the starting point. This is a circular hole in one of the rocks that lie in shelves across the Quoich Water. There is a tradition that in 1715 the Earl's men met at the linn, poured 'ankers of potent Aquavitae' into the Punch Bowl, and drank toasts to the Jacobite cause. The 'bowl' must have had a bottom to it then, for nothing potent comes out of it now. Water, not whisky, pours through the hole as the burn rushes towards the Dee. Apart from its missing bottom, the 'bowl' is perfectly formed, and its shape is best seen when the burn is low.

From the parking area at Allanaquoich, the Linn is only a short distance up the burn, past a red-roofed cottage that is now boarded up. The grass slopes here can be slippery in wet weather, so take care. The cottage on the right near the bridge was known as Queen Victoria's Tea Room, and later as the Princess's Tea Room after Victoria's granddaughter, the Princess Royal, who

INFORMATION

Distance: 14km (9 miles) circular.

Start and Finish: Linn of Quoich. From Braemar take the Linn of Dee road and continue to Linn of Quoich (15km/9 miles in total), where there is informal parking near the bridge.

Terrain: Generally good paths and tracks, but a rough, narrow path in Clais Fhearnaig. Boots recommended. Take waterproof and warm clothing with you and OS Landranger sheet 43.

Refreshments: None on route. Take food and drink with you.

Toilets: At the Linn of Dee car park.

The Punchbowl at Glen Quoich

married the Duke of Fife, former owner of Mar Lodge. For a long time the cottage was in a ruinous condition, but it has now been restored.

A wooden bridge spans the Quoich near the Punch Bowl. It was built in recent years by Scotrail volunteers, replacing a bridge which was on the point of collapse. It provides access to the Punch Bowl from the right (west) bank of the burn and also takes you to a path which links up with the main track going up the Quoich Water by the route you are taking.

The Linn, shaded by larch and birch trees, is an idyllic spot. The water flows over a blue-green schist which gives it a lovely translucent colour. Its 'big brother' on the Dee may be more spectacular, but the Linn of Quoich has it for beauty.

Follow the path uphill to the main track, which comes up on your left from the road. Turn right, and you are setting out through what Seton Gordon, the distinguished naturalist and writer, called "one of the most delightful glens of the Cairngorms". He gave its name as Gleann Cuaich, the glen of the wooden cup. Some people link this with the rocky quaich or bowl at the Linn, but not all the experts agree.

When you are well up the glen, the great mass of Beinn a'Bhuird comes into view, with the thin finger of a path climbing up over its shoulder. Your route, however, is not to the high tops, but into Clais Fhearnaig, the hidden glen, a pass or ravine lying between Glen Quoich and Glen Lui.

The turning-off point is where the forestry plantation on the left comes to an end, about 5 km from the Linn of Quoich. Look for a burn that is carried under the track by two large pipes. This is the Allt Clais Fhearnaig, the burn that will lead you through the pass to Glen Lui.

Clais Fhearnaig, linking Glen Quoich and Glen Lui

Immediately across the burn, turn left up a path which leads to a small fenced-in field with a rough shed in one corner. The path goes up hill beside the left-hand fence of the field. As you near the top of the fence, the path goes off at a '10 o'clock' angle and crosses a grassy area, keeping parallel with the forestry plantation over on the left.

Drop down into a hollow where a small loch can be seen. The name Clais Fhearnaig actually means 'hollow of the place of alders', although another interpretation is 'the little glen'. This ravine or cut in the hills is part of a great geological fault running across Scotland. At one time a series of small, rushy pools lay in the hollow. When trout were seen in them many years ago, it was decided to dam the water and make an artificial loch for trout fishing. Trout can still be seen louping from the loch today.

Down by the loch you are cut off from the outside world. Ahead, it looks as if there is no way out. Stunted tree trunks form intricate patterns on the surface and rushes poke slender green fingers up through the water. The 'little glen' is a tranquil place, with only the occasional walker disturbing the peace.

The path pushes along the loch's edge towards what appears to be a dead-end, but as it begins to climb gently uphill another tiny, rush-strewn lochan appears. Beyond it, the moorland opens up and the path, clinging to the hill on the right, heads down into Glen Lui. As you descend you will see the old larachs that are scattered along the glen, a reminder of the days before depopulation. With luck, you will also see the great herds of deer that graze beside the Lui Water.

The path crosses a small burn and descends easily to the Derry Lodge track. When you reach the track, turn left along Glen Lui to the Black Bridge. Don't cross the bridge, but go past it and turn up the track going through the woods of Doire Bhraghad (as in Walk 23).

Stick strictly to this track, ignoring any paths going off to the left or right, and it will eventually, in about 3km, take you down to the road at Claybokie. Turn left and you have an easy 4km stroll back to the car park at Linn of Quoich.

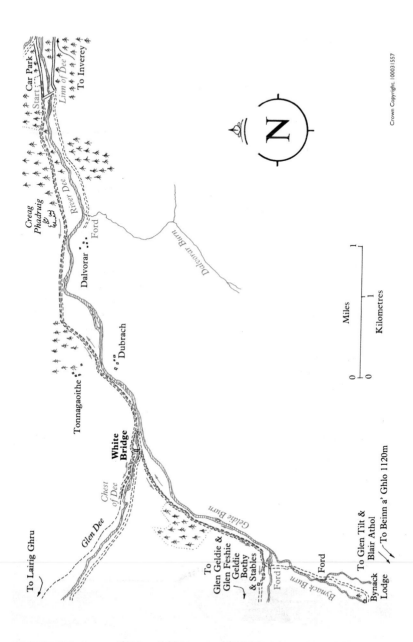

Crown Copyright: 100031557

WHITE BRIDGE

Two great passes come together at the White Bridge in Glen Dee. One is the Lairig Ghru leading north to Strathspey, and the other is the pass through Glen Tilt to Blair Atholl. This walk takes you to the junction of the two passes, and gives you a peep into both.

From the Linn of Dee car park, walk back along the road to the Linn and continue straight ahead on the track. There is a sign pointing the way to the Lairig Ghru, Glen Geldie and Glen Tilt, and a reminder that you are entering wild and remote country.

The track going west to the White Bridge is fringed by pine trees, but those on the left quickly give way to open moorland. The trees on the right hug the track for about 1.5 km, rising up the slopes below Craig Phadruig. Eagles have been known to nest in this pine belt, within a kilometre of the picnic parties and tourist coaches at the Linn.

On the opposite bank of the Dee another track can be seen, but it runs out at a ford across the Dee where the Dalvorar Burn comes down from the hills. There are ruins of old settlements on both sides of the river, and those at Dalvorar have a small place in the history books. Dalvorar is from the Gaelic Dail a'Mhorair,

INFORMATION

Distance: 16km (10 miles) circular.

Start and Finish: Linn of Dee, 10km (6 miles) west of Braemar. There is a large car park near the bridge (current charge £2).

Terrain: Good tracks or paths all the way, but boots are recommended. Take waterproof and warm clothing with you.

Refreshments: None on route. Take food and drink with you.

Toilets: At the car park at Linn of Dee.

The White Bridge

the 'haugh of the nobleman', but which nobleman gave his name to it nobody knows. Perhaps it was Viscount Dundee, who is said to have camped here with his troops 14 days before the Battle of Killiecrankie in July 1689.

Here, too, the swollen Dee raged across the glen in the floods of 1829, known as the Muckle Spate. The waters swept around the farmhouse at Dalvorar so quickly that the farmer, his wife and seven children barely had time to make their escape. They waded away from their home and tramped through the storm to Inverey. Today, the spates still come, as the warning notice at the Linn of Dee reminds us, but they are seldom as angry as the Muckle Spate of 1829.

One ruin on the right of the track has the name of Tonnagaoithe. It is supposed to come from the Gaelic Ton na Gaoithe, meaning 'bottom of the wind', but Dr Adam Watson and Elizabeth Allan, in their book *The Place Names of Upper Deeside*, give a ruder translation. They say it was 'translated to us as "winy airse", which is Scots for "windy arse"'.

On the south side of the river, 3 km from the Linn of Dee, are the remains of Dubrach, which also has historical associations. 'Dubrach' was the by-name of Peter

Chest of Dee

Grant, the oldest rebel in the 1745 Jacobite Rising, whose father was a tenant of the farm in Glen Dee. Peter lived to be 110 years old and, ironically, was given a pension by King George IV. They say that when 'Dubrach' was buried in Braemar kirkyard, four gallons of whisky were drunk 'even before the lifting'.

The farm of Dubrach was also the setting for one of Upper Deeside's most baffling mysteries. After the 1745 Rising, a guard of Hanoverian soldiers under the command of Sergeant Arthur Davies was quartered at the farm. In September 1749, while on his way to Altanour in Glen Ey, Sgt Davies disappeared. The following year his body was found in the Glen Ey area.

The White Bridge spans the Dee about a kilometre past Dubrach. The track across it goes south by the Geldie Burn, whereas straight ahead the path continues towards the Lairig Ghru and on to Rothiemurchus and Aviemore. About 700m along this track is the Chest of Dee, where the river flows over a series of rock shelves above clear, deep pools. The Chest, or Kist, which is well worth a detour, can also be reached by a footpath on the opposite side of the river. The picturesque pools can be seen from either side, but the Lairig Ghru path is the best place from which to take photographs.

From the Chest of Dee you look up to the Devil's Point and the mouth of the Lairig Ghru, while back at the White Bridge the Geldie draws you down towards Bynack and Glen Tilt. So here the two great passes lie to each side of you – the Lairig Ghru, which the writer H.V. Morton described as 'an early Italian painter's idea of hell', and Glen Tilt, which Thomas Pennant said was 'the most dangerous and most horrible I have ever travelled'.

Today the White Bridge is a black, wooden structure mounted on steel girders, although it was said to be painted white at one time. Oddly enough the Gaelic name for the Geldie is *geal dhe*, the White Dee. Cross the bridge and follow the track as it runs between the Geldie Burn and a plantation of trees on your right.

Bynack stables at Glen Geldie

This was a well-beaten drovers' path and if events had taken a different turn it might have become a motor road from Strathspey to Deeside. In the 18th century, General George Wade contemplated a road link from Ruthven Barracks, near Kingussie, through Glen Feshie and Glen Geldie to Braemar, and his 20th century successors also had a dream in their minds of a fast tourist highway from west to east. Happily, nothing came of it.

The Geldie comes bouncing in from the west. The track turns right to Glen Geldie and Glen Feshie, passing a ruined red-roofed building, all that is left of the Lower Geldie cottage and stables. Across from the cottage, broken pillars mark the site of the former bridge over the Geldie. Now, walkers going south through Glen Tilt (or coming the other way) have to cross by fording the river, which in winter can be ravaged by the spates that brought the bridge down.

From the ford a cluster of trees can be seen across the river about 1.5km away. They shelter the ruins of Bynack Lodge, where Queen Victoria stopped for tea on her way back to Balmoral from Blair Atholl. The Lodge was said at one time to be haunted by a poltergeist.

From the Geldie stables you can look down Glen Tilt and see mighty Beinn a'Ghlo rising up in the distance. It will be your last view before you turn and head back to the White Bridge and the track to Linn of Dee.

INDEX